A TEACHER'S GUIDE TO STANDARDS-BASED LEARNING

foreword by Robert J. Marzano

TAMMY HEFLEBOWER, JAN K. HOEGH,
PHILIP B. WARRICK, & JEFF FLYGARE

MARZANO
Resources

555 North Morton Street
Bloomington, IN 47404
888.849.0851
FAX: 866.801.1477

email: info@MarzanoResources.com
MarzanoResources.com

Visit **MarzanoResources.com/reproducibles** to download the free reproducibles in this book.

Printed in the United States of America

Library of Congress Control Number: 2018941178

ISBN: 978-1-943360-25-3

Editorial Director: Sarah Payne-Mills
Art Director: Rian Anderson
Managing Production Editor: Kendra Slayton
Production Editor: Alissa Voss
Senior Editor: Amy Rubenstein
Copy Editor: Ashante K. Thomas
Proofreader: Evie Madsen
Text Designer: Laura Cox
Editorial Assistant: Sarah Ludwig

Table of Contents

About the Authors

 **Tammy Heflebower, EdD,** is a highly sought-after school leader and consultant with vast experience in urban, rural, and suburban districts throughout the United States, Australia, Canada, Denmark, England, and the Netherlands. Dr. Heflebower has served as an award-winning classroom teacher, building leader, district leader, regional professional development director, and national and international trainer. She has also been an adjunct professor of curriculum, instruction, and assessment at several universities, and a prominent member and leader of numerous statewide and national educational organizations. Dr. Heflebower was the vice president and then senior scholar at Marzano Resources prior to becoming the CEO of her own company, !nspire Inc: Education and Business Solutions. She also specializes in powerful presentation and facilitation techniques—writing and sharing them worldwide.

Dr. Heflebower is widely published. She is lead author of the award-winning book *A School Leader's Guide to Standards-Based Grading* and is coauthor of *Collaborative Teams That Transform Schools: The Next Step in PLCs* and *Teaching & Assessing 21st Century Skills.* She is a contributor to *A Handbook for High Reliability Schools: The Next Step in School Reform, Becoming a Reflective Teacher, Coaching Classroom Instruction, The Highly Engaged Classroom, The Principal as Assessment Leader, The Teacher as Assessment Leader,* and *Using Common Core Standards to Enhance Classroom Instruction & Assessment.* Her articles have been featured in *Kappan, Educational Leadership, Diversity Journal, Education Week* blog, and the *Nebraska Council of School Administrators Today.*

Dr. Heflebower holds a bachelor of arts from Hastings College in Hastings, Nebraska, where she was honored as an Outstanding Young Alumna and her team was inducted into the hall of fame. She has a master of arts from the University of Nebraska Omaha. She also earned an educational administrative endorsement and a doctor of education in educational administration from the University of Nebraska–Lincoln.

Jan K. Hoegh has been an educator for thirty-plus years and an author and associate for Marzano Resources since 2010. Prior to joining the Marzano team, she was a classroom teacher, building-level leader, professional development specialist, assistant high school principal, curriculum coordinator, and most recently assistant director of statewide assessment for the Nebraska Department of Education, where her primary focus was Nebraska State Accountability test development. Hoegh has served on a variety of statewide and national standards and assessment committees and has presented at numerous conferences around the world.

As an associate with Marzano Resources, Hoegh works with educators around the world as they strive to improve student achievement. Her passion for education, combined with extensive knowledge of curriculum, instruction, and assessment, provides credible support for teachers, leaders, schools, and districts. A primary training focus for Hoegh is high-quality classroom assessment and grading practices. She is a coauthor of the books *Collaborative Teams That Transform Schools* and *A School Leader's Guide to Standards-Based Grading*, as well as other publications.

Hoegh holds a bachelor of arts in elementary education and a master of arts in educational administration, both from the University of Nebraska at Kearney. She also earned a specialization in assessment from the University of Nebraska–Lincoln.

Philip B. Warrick, EdD, spent the first twenty-five years of his education career as a teacher, assistant principal, principal, and superintendent and has experience in leading schools in the states of Nebraska and Texas. Dr. Warrick was named 1998 Nebraska Outstanding New Principal of the Year and was the 2005 Nebraska State High School Principal of the Year. He is a past regional president for the Nebraska Council of School Administrators (NCSA) and also served on the NCSA legislative committee. In 2003, he was one of the initial participants to attend the Nebraska Educational Leadership Institute, conducted by the Gallup Corporation at Gallup University in Omaha. In 2008, Dr. Warrick was hired as the campus principal at Round Rock High School in Round Rock, Texas. In 2010, he was invited to be an inaugural participant in the Texas Principals' Visioning Institute, where he collaborated with other principals from the state of Texas to develop a vision for effective practices in Texas schools.

Dr. Warrick has coauthored *A School Leader's Guide to Standards-Based Grading*, *Collaborative Teams That Transform Schools*, *A Handbook for High Reliability Schools*, and *Leading a High Reliability School*. Dr. Warrick joined the Solution Tree–Marzano Resources team in 2011 and works as an author and global consultant in the areas of school leadership, curriculum, instruction, assessment, grading, and collaborative teaming. He earned a bachelor of science from Chadron State College in Chadron, Nebraska, and earned master's and doctoral degrees from the University of Nebraska–Lincoln.

 **Jeff Flygare** is a former classroom teacher, English department chair, professional developer, and building-level leader. During his twenty-six-year career teaching high school English, he taught nearly every course in the department. Flygare developed classes in mythology, Shakespeare, philosophy, and comparative religions, and worked with social studies colleagues to create an interdisciplinary class called World Studies, which he team-taught successfully for seventeen years. He taught Advanced Placement (AP) English classes for twenty-one years and served as an AP English literature reader and table leader for Educational Testing Service for many years. He adopted standards-based learning in his classroom and successfully taught students at all levels in a standards-based environment for many years.

Flygare also has a strong theatrical background, working first as an actor and then as a director at a major regional theater company in Colorado. He directed many high school productions, both traditional and Shakespearean, as well. As a Marzano Resources associate, Flygare travels around the world to work with educators on topics involving curriculum, instruction, and assessment. He is the author of *Close Reading in the Secondary Classroom*.

He holds a bachelor's degree in English from the State University of New York–Buffalo, a master's degree in English from the University of Colorado–Denver, and a master's degree in education with an endorsement in gifted education from the University of Colorado–Colorado Springs.

Foreword

by Robert J. Marzano

For decades, educators have been discussing standards-based assessment and grading. Indeed, as far back as the early 1990s, I and others were writing quite extensively about the impact the standards movement was likely to have on K–12 schooling. In this new book, Heflebower, Hoegh, Warrick, and Flygare revisit some of those topics but add the perspective of how standards should affect both teaching and learning. At the core of their discussions and recommendations are proficiency scales.

While the term *proficiency scales* is used in many different ways and has many different manifestations, the type of scale used by the authors goes back to my early work in the 1990s and is currently being used in every U.S. state, and a number of countries, to one degree or another. Such proficiency scales have been well vetted regarding their utility with assessment, grading, curriculum, and instruction.

To design this particular type of proficiency scale, educators must identify those topics from state or local standards that are essential for students' academic success. The authors refer to this process as *prioritizing the standards*. The content within each of the essential topics derived from prioritized standards is then organized into a progression of knowledge embedded within the proficiency scale, which becomes the guaranteed curriculum within a school or district.

After establishing a firm foundation regarding the nature of and need for proficiency scales, the authors address how the scales can and should be used. First, and perhaps foremost, proficiency scales should be highly visible. Teachers should make students aware of the essential topics that they will address throughout the year and the content in the proficiency scales for each topic. This renders the curriculum completely transparent for students and parents. They know what will be taught throughout year, when it will be taught, and precisely what proficiency looks like for each topic.

Each proficiency scale also governs assessment. In fact, it is ideal if cooperative teams within the professional learning communities (PLC) process generate common pretests and posttests using the proficiency scales. Better yet, teachers in a collaborative team can score students' pretests and posttests to determine individual student needs and calibrate the manner in which teachers design and score assessments based on proficiency scales.

Teachers should ask students to set goals regarding their learning of the content in specific proficiency scales. A powerful addendum to this process is encouraging students to track their progress over time on specific proficiency scales. In this way, both their current status and their growth can be the subject of celebration.

Classroom instruction and the planning of that instruction should be based on the proficiency scales addressed within a unit. The authors demonstrate that proficiency scales can serve this need regardless of the specific instructional model that a school or district uses. Grading and reporting should also revolve around scores on proficiency scales. The authors illustrate how teachers can translate standards-based student scores into traditional letter grades and percentage scores.

These are only a few of the issues the authors address in *A Teacher's Guide to Standards-Based Learning.* Those readers familiar with standards-based education will recognize many topics but will surely find a fresh perspective on each. Those new to standards-based education will receive a clear picture of what it might look at the classroom level and from the perspective of the student.

Introduction

Schools changing instructional and assessment practices to accommodate new standards means many teachers are required to make what they often consider a major transition in their teaching. For many teachers, this transition comes after years of successful teaching in a familiar, comfortable format, with content they know well. It may feel as though they're shifting over to the latest hot topic in education, and the last thing in the world they want to do is move away from teaching methods, policies, and practices that have served them well for their entire careers.

Some teachers may have a substantial philosophical issue with the whole notion of teaching to standards. They may have entered the teaching profession because of their love of the content and with a strong desire to share that passion with their students. In fact, they've been doing just that for many years, and their students light up when their teacher "does her thing"! Now, with this new concept of teaching, they face the need to change. Will it be a positive change? Will it be stressful? Will they be successful?

Yes to all three.

It may appear that the only obvious outcome of this transition is the associated stress for teachers. Change is never easy, and shifting to standards-based learning won't be either. So, if teachers are going to go through the stress of these changes, it ought to be for very good reasons. Let's start by examining some of these reasons.

One of our authors, Jeff Flygare, taught in a traditional classroom for over twenty years before transitioning to standards-based learning. The following is his message to teachers facing the change to standards-based learning.

First, understand that I know how you feel. Before changing to standards-based learning, I had taught as a traditional English language arts teacher, using traditional instruction and grading practices, for twenty-one years. I was very successful. My students learned the content, and they returned to my classroom to take additional classes from me often. It was working for me, yet I took on standards-based learning without anyone telling me I had to. Why? Because, as good as I was, I knew I wasn't reaching all my students. When I looked at changing my instruction, assessment, and grading practice, I knew that my best students would still learn under the new system, but I thought perhaps with standards-based learning, which promised more student involvement with and commitment to their own learning, I might reach more of my students. And that was exactly what I found to be true.

I shifted to standards-based learning over one weekend in August just before the new school year started. I figured out the basics of standards-based learning, found a way to make our very traditional online gradebook report standards-based scores, and rolled it out with my new students on the first day of school. They had no idea what standards-based learning was, so I committed as much time as they wanted to take during the first thirty days of the school year to explain how this new instruction and assessment system worked. They had lots of questions. I covered the same ground with them many times in that thirty days, but eventually they began to get the idea that I would have standards in the classroom, that instruction would focus on those standards, and that they would be expected to gradually reach proficiency on those standards.

I was sure I could explain the system to them given enough time. But I never expected the sudden (within thirty days) and profound change in their attitude toward their own learning that manifested itself in front of me every school day! The entire conversation in the classroom changed. In a highly competitive and high-performing high school, where most of my students would go on to college, the focus of my students went, almost immediately, off grades. They began to talk with me and each other about what they knew and what they were learning, and how they were doing on the learning progression to proficiency on each standard.

This will happen with your students. It may not happen as fast as it did with mine. But stay tuned into their conversations as you begin to practice standards-based learning and be ready to catch your jaw when it drops. The most important change you will see is the way in which your students begin to accept responsibility for their own learning. There will also be some additional benefits. Homework completion may increase. Enthusiasm about the content may increase. Apathy may decrease. And you will find yourself creating many more lifelong learners than you have been.

I realize how difficult it is to believe until you see it happen. But be open to it, and, most importantly, give standards-based learning a legitimate try. Don't try it for two weeks, or two months. Give it a couple of school years. And really try it. Don't leave something (like student goal setting) out. Do it all. Do it at your own pace, but do it all. Then, be objective about what you see and what you don't see.

There is even more good news. While standards-based learning is better for students, in fact, once teachers make it through the transition stage to full implementation, standards-based learning is better for teachers. It provides time to go deeper, clarity about the content, and evidence that they are reaching more students.

A Necessary Paradigm Shift

Standards-based learning will require some fundamental paradigm shifts, but these shifts won't mean teaching in a completely different and unfamiliar way. When standards-based learning is happening in the classroom, the content taught won't change very much. Even the teaching strategies that teachers use won't change much. But how teachers think about *what* and *how* they teach will change profoundly.

Perhaps the biggest paradigm shift for the teacher in the classroom is moving away from the notion that there is a substantial amount of content to work through in a school year and toward the notion that there is a set of standards, including factual knowledge and sets of skills, that he or she must develop in students. The content is there as the *vehicle* to develop those standards. The sequence of dealing with the content will likely be very similar to what has been traditionally taught, but its purpose will be different.

While curriculum and instruction will be very similar, the one area that will change a great deal will be assessments. Now, instead of assessing specific content in, say, a unit test, the unit test will assess certain standards by asking students to use the content they've learned to show their growth on the standards. This is a subtle but powerful difference.

Essential to standards-based learning is the use of the standards to identify, for teachers, students, and parents, what the students must *know* and be able to *do* by the end of the learning. This places what happens in the students' heads at the center of everything pedagogical in the classroom. Teachers are looking to change the students' knowledge and abilities through their actions. This represents a change from traditional teaching. Traditionally, teachers design instruction to present content to students that they expect them to learn. In standards-based learning, they design instruction to promote student learning of the standards through the content. The good news is that standards-based learning, in placing the student's learning at the center of what happens in the classroom, is a much more effective method for accomplishing the teacher's new educational task—helping every student learn.

One major focus of standards-based learning is to achieve an integrated model of learning. Because the standards will sit at the center of everything teachers do in the classroom, identifying and clarifying those standards properly will integrate everything teachers do. Therefore, standards-based learning is a highly effective method of connecting curriculum, instruction, assessment, and feedback.

A result of this alignment for teachers who have taught in a traditional setting for a very long time is that, once the transition to standards-based is made, a clarity emerges that often wasn't there before. Importantly, that clarity will emerge for students as well. For perhaps the first time in their experience of school, they will see the relevance of everything teachers ask them to do, and they will be much more likely to participate in the learning because they are motivated to watch their own progress.

A Word About Terminology

In this book, we use the term *standards-based learning* rather than *standards-based grading* because the program involves so much more than assigning students grades. One important aspect of standards-based learning is that with standards as the focus of curriculum, instruction, assessment, and feedback, the grades students receive are meaningful to them in terms of their own learning.

Two terms that this book uses interchangeably throughout, though our primary usage will focus on the latter, are *standards referenced* and *standards based*. This occurs because the process for figuring grades in each concept is essentially the same. However, there is a difference between the terms, as can be seen in a review of literature on these two topics.

Standards referenced means that teachers report student progress in reference to the priority standards for a specific grade level or course (Marzano, 2010). Grant Wiggins (1993, 1996) and Robert J. Marzano (2010) describe *standards-referenced grading* as a system in which teachers give students feedback about their proficiency on a set of defined standards and schools report students' levels of performance on the grade-level standards, but students advance at the end of the course or year based on passing performance and other factors, only some of which may involve proficiency on the standards. Marzano (2010) observed, "The vast majority of schools and districts that claim to have standards-based systems in fact have standards-referenced systems" (pp. 18–19). In a system of standards-referenced grading and reporting, students might move upward in grade or content level without demonstrating proficiency in all the standards for that particular course or grade level.

Standards-based grading is a system of assessing and reporting that describes student progress in relation to standards. In a standards-based system, a student can demonstrate mastery of a set of standards and move immediately to a more challenging set of standards. This means that if a third-grade student masters the entire set of third-grade mathematics standards in two months, that student immediately begins to work on fourth-grade mathematics standards. The same principle applies to all grade levels and subject areas: as soon as a student demonstrates competency with all the standards for a specific level and subject area, he or she immediately begins working on the next level of standards for that subject area. At the same time, a student who does not achieve proficiency on the standards continues to work on those standards until he or she reaches proficiency. Thus, standards-based grading is the process teachers also use for *competency-based* or *proficiency-based learning and reporting*.

For the purpose of our work and this book, we will use the term *standards-based learning* to represent the practices and processes we explain. However, we will refer to *standards-referenced reporting* when appropriate during our discussion of traditional methods of grading and delivering report cards.

How to Use This Book

While it is true that there are resources for administrators and school leaders involved with the change to standards-based learning, we want to provide a resource for the K–12 classroom teacher who has to make standards-based learning work in his or her classroom. While we present the theory behind standards-based learning, this book's purpose is to provide practical guidance for the classroom teacher. We base the information we present in these pages on our years of training classroom teachers around the world in their transition to this new concept of teaching.

Our approach is sequential, and we present each stage of adopting and implementing standards-based learning. In each chapter, teachers will find specific advice and examples designed to make the transition easier.

Chapter 1 discusses how to plan instruction in a standards-based learning environment using proficiency scales. This chapter provides detailed guidance on how to understand the learning progressions within proficiency scales. It then discusses how teachers can use their proficiency scales to create and sequence cohesive lesson and unit plans to optimize student learning.

In chapter 2, teachers will then learn how to instruct their classes using proficiency scales. Special mention is made of instruction techniques to use when beginning content instruction, as students develop proficiency, and when students move past proficiency.

Chapter 3 outlines the crucial student practice of setting goals and tracking their own progress toward these goals. It provides strategies for how teachers can encourage, both implicitly and explicitly, goal-setting behaviors in their students and highlight goals that will best encourage student learning. Finally, this chapter contains ways for teachers and students to track progress both individually and classwide, as well as suggestions for celebrating success as they reach goals.

Chapter 4 thoroughly explains how to administer quality classroom assessments in a standards-based environment, and how to subsequently figure student grades. We present types of assessments and different scoring methods, as well as strategies for calculating summative scores using proficiency scales and dealing with unusual patterns of performance.

Special considerations for teaching exceptional students is the topic of chapter 5. This chapter provides guidance for using and modifying proficiency scales with exceptional learners, such as students with disabilities, English learners (ELs), and gifted learners. It also discusses how to link standards-based grading with special classes such as Advanced Placement (AP) and International Baccalaureate (IB) classes.

Finally, chapter 6 delves into how to best communicate the standards-based system of grading to parents and other community members. It details how to approach parent-teacher conferences, including student-led conferences; how to convey proficiency scale grades on report cards; and how to convert standards-based grading methods to letter or percentage grades, when required. A list of frequently asked questions can be found in appendix A for additional information on implementation of standards-based learning practices.

While not a step-by-step guide, this book tries to provide the basic information most teachers can use as a starting point to adapt their instructional program to their specific needs. We will provide the overall framework, specifically advising where we think teachers must implement elements and suggesting places where they can adapt elements. In the end, you as the teacher must make the program your own. We hope we can provide the advice and benefit of our experience for your journey.

1

Planning Instruction With Proficiency Scales

When planning instruction within a standards-based learning environment, it is important for teachers to understand that the focus of instruction will evolve from a content-centered approach to one that develops student knowledge and abilities on the standards. Instead of forming the knowledge the student will need to acquire throughout the unit, the content is now the vehicle that drives student knowledge and skills development. Proficiency scales serve as a starting point to develop a plan that guides student growth on the standards.

This chapter provides teachers with a comprehensive understanding of how to create and use proficiency scales in a standards-based environment. It will explain how teachers can plan instruction by prioritizing standards, assessing students' initial placement with a preassessment, and creating well-sequenced unit and lesson plans. This process is easily adapted to any instructional framework the teacher may be using.

Identifying Priority and Supporting Standards

Before discussing proficiency scales in detail, we should define the terms *priority* and *supporting standards*. Educators are tasked with teaching a large array of state standards, but a quick examination of these standards by an experienced teacher reveals that not all of these standards are of equal importance. Marzano (2003) has shown that there is insufficient instructional time in the K–12 years to bring all students to proficiency on every required state standard. Teachers must thus determine the priority of standards so that they can focus their instructional time on those standards identified as essential to a particular class or grade level. The remaining standards, which educators still teach but for which students may or may not reach proficiency, are identified as *supporting standards*.

In general, districts provide teachers tasked with implementing standards-based learning in their classrooms with lists of priority standards. If it is necessary to go through the process of identifying priority standards, more information about this process can be found in *A School Leader's Guide to Standards-Based Grading* (Heflebower, Hoegh, & Warrick, 2014).

It is important to note that *priority standards* are the ones on which teachers focus instruction, assessment, and feedback in standards-based learning. Supporting standards are still taught, and may or may not be assessed, but the priority standards are the basis of assessing and reporting student performance. Thus, because teachers need proficiency scales for planning and delivering instruction, creating assessments, and reporting progress, we will create proficiency scales only for priority standards. Proficiency scales are usually not needed for supporting standards.

Understanding Proficiency Scales

Standards-based learning emerges from a teacher's thorough understanding of the concept of proficiency scales (first created by Robert J. Marzano; for more information see Marzano, 2006). In essence, a proficiency scale defines a learning progression or set of learning goals for a specific topic, relative to a given standard. It shows teachers and students what proficiency looks like, what knowledge and skills students need to achieve proficiency, and how students might go beyond proficiency. See figure 1.1 for the generic form of a proficiency scale.

Score	Description
4.0	Advanced content
3.0	Target content
2.0	Simpler content necessary for proficiency
1.0	With help, partial success with score 2.0 content and score 3.0 content
0.0	Even with help, no success

Source: © 2007 by Marzano & Associates; Marzano, 2010, p. 45.

Figure 1.1: Generic form of a proficiency scale.

Score 3.0 is the heart of the proficiency scale; it defines the target content that teachers expect all students to know and be able to do. When creating a proficiency scale, teachers place the standard or other statement of expectations at score 3.0. Score 2.0 describes simpler content—the foundational knowledge and skills that students will need to master before progressing to proficiency. This often includes vocabulary and basic facts. Score 4.0 provides students the opportunity to go above and beyond expectations by applying their knowledge in new situations or demonstrating understanding beyond what the teacher teaches in class. Score 1.0 and score 0.0 do not involve specific content. Score 1.0 indicates that a student can demonstrate some knowledge or skill with help from the teacher, but not independently. Score 0.0 means that, even with help, a student cannot show any understanding. Figure 1.2 depicts a sample proficiency scale as a teacher might use it in a classroom—with specific content for a certain topic and grade level.

Score 4.0	The student will solve an engineering problem involving decisions about which material, based on its properties, will best satisfy a set of requirements and constraints.
Score 3.5	In addition to score 3.0 performance, partial success at score 4.0 content
Score 3.0	The student will classify materials based on their properties (magnetism, conductivity, density, solubility, boiling point, melting point).
Score 2.5	No major errors or omissions regarding score 2.0 content, and partial success at score 3.0 content
Score 2.0	Student will recognize and recall basic vocabulary, such as *magnetism, conductivity, density, solubility, boiling point,* and *melting point.* Students will perform basic processes, such as: • Making observations to identify the properties of a material • Taking measurements to identify the properties of a material
Score 1.5	Partial success at score 2.0 content, and major errors or omissions regarding score 3.0 content
Score 1.0	With help, the student will achieve partial success at score 2.0 content and score 3.0 content.
Score 0.5	With help, partial success at score 2.0 content but not at score 3.0 content
Score 0.0	Even with help, the student has no success.

Source: Adapted from Marzano, Norford, Finn, & Finn, 2017, p. 29.

Figure 1.2: Proficiency scale for a fifth-grade science topic.

The scale in figure 1.2 defines a learning progression for the fifth-grade science topic of material properties. Score 3.0 describes the learning target that all students have to reach, score 2.0 describes foundational vocabulary and processes, and score 4.0 describes an advanced task. In some scales, score 4.0 may simply state that students will demonstrate in-depth inferences and applications, rather than specifying a task.

The scale in figure 1.2 also includes half-point scores. This helps teachers measure student knowledge more precisely and helps students see their progress and inspires them to keep working. Students who receive a half-point score have demonstrated knowledge that is between two levels. Score 3.5 means that a student has demonstrated proficiency and had partial success with advanced content, score 2.5 means that a student has mastered the simpler content and demonstrated some understanding of the target content, and so on.

In a standards-based learning environment, proficiency scales form the basis of instruction, assessment, feedback, and grading. Teachers deliver instruction based on the expectations and progressions that proficiency scales define. Assessments align with scales, and students receive feedback on their performance that clearly describes where they are on the scale. Teachers report grades on the four-point scale. The proficiency scale forms the foundation for a consistent system centered around student learning. Principal William Barnes describes proficiency scales and their impact in his school:

> In our standards-based grading system, standards outline what students should learn, and our scales clearly define what students need to know and be able to do to achieve each level of knowledge. Since these standards and scales inform our grades and form the foundations of our courses, it is much easier to purposefully align our whole instructional system. The activities and assessments that represent the day-to-day work in our classes are aligned to the standards and scales, so teachers and students are able to communicate progress and learning in a clear and concise way. This results in a much richer understanding of where gaps in learning exist, while also providing an opportunity for teachers to push students who are more advanced in their learning. (Personal communication, January 19, 2018)

Since teachers share proficiency scales with students throughout instruction, these scales become the common language surrounding everything that happens in the classroom. This has the added advantage of connecting students and teachers with the learning that will occur across the unit, raising students' ability to understand the relevance of each lesson, activity, assignment, and assessment in the unit. The scale becomes the centerpiece of communication and understanding in the classroom, as well as the common language for discussing learning between teacher and student (see figure 1.3).

Figure 1.3: The role of the proficiency scale in classroom communication and understanding.

Given this understanding of the proficiency scale and its role as the basis of instruction, assessment, feedback, and grading, we will now discuss how teachers can adapt the standards-based paradigm to their desired teaching framework. The following section will discuss how to plan standards-based instruction using *The New Art and Science of*

Teaching framework and how this method can be adapted to other teaching frameworks the teacher may be using.

Planning Standards-Based Instruction

Teachers new to standards-based learning may find a focus on the standards rather than content to be uncomfortable at first. Traditionally, the sequence of presenting content to students has been the guide for instructional planning. As teachers consider the planning process for standards-based learning, the content moves into a secondary position. That content will still be there, and likely in much the same sequence. But the starting place for planning instruction will be the priority standards and their associated proficiency scales.

Further, no matter what instructional framework a teacher uses, he or she can adopt standards-based instruction to the framework requirements. There are multiple frameworks available to teachers, including:

- Danielson Framework for Teaching (Danielson, 2007)

- ADDIE model (www.instructionaldesign.org/models/addie.html)

- The Dick and Carey Method (Kurt, n.d.)

- Madeline Hunter's Instructional Theory Into Practice (Wilson, n.d.)

- Marzano's (2017) *The New Art and Science of Teaching* framework

- The Framework for Intentional and Targeted Teaching (FIT Teaching™; Fisher, Frey, & Hite, 2016)

While some of these frameworks put the teacher's focus more at the lesson level than the unit level, in a standards-based classroom, students make gains in knowledge and skills across large units of instruction. Thus, in a standards-based classroom, the focus of the teacher in matching an instructional framework to a set of priority standards is to design instruction that starts where the students' knowledge and abilities are on the standard and ends with proficiency on those standards. For example, in the Danielson framework (Danielson, 2007), a teacher designing a standards-based unit will address the role of standards throughout Domain 1: Planning and Preparation, as well as specifically in Domain 3: Instruction. For the purposes of this book, we will use *The New Art and Science of Teaching* framework as the example, but the cognitive processes involved in designing standards-based learning work equally well within any applicable instructional framework.

Through the lens of *The New Art and Science of Teaching* framework, we will now discuss sequencing standards within the unit, creating the unit plan, and differentiating with response to intervention (RTI).

Sequencing Standards in the Unit

In the shift to standards-based learning, teachers discover quickly that unit plans are the focus of understanding the development of the priority standards' knowledge and skills. While lesson planning remains important, and teachers use instructional strategies at the lesson level, the vision of student learning should start at the unit level.

Traditionally, units have been the logical way in which teachers break down content into small chunks that they can teach and assess. In a standards-based system, units function in the same way, though the purpose is to break down the development of the knowledge and skills that the standards require into smaller segments. An example may help clarify this idea.

Consider an English language arts (ELA) teacher planning the sequence of units for a year of eighth-grade ELA. Traditionally, there are large categories of content that she will teach, such as writing, reading, vocabulary, grammar, and perhaps some other important content. In a traditional approach, there are a number of ways in which to group this content. One effective way is to organize the content by theme, allowing the teacher to group works of literature by large thematic categories and to connect writing instruction and vocabulary to that literature study. Grammar will find its way in, perhaps with the literature or writing, or perhaps as a separate chunk of content done each week through the year. Another way to traditionally group the content is by genre. This has the advantage of sequencing the literature in terms of its challenge for students. In this case, the teacher would likely start with less challenging forms of literature, such as the short story, and then proceed to larger, more challenging works. Drama might follow, then the novel, and finally the most challenging form, poetry. Writing, vocabulary, and grammar would accompany this general sequence. Either approach, or another based on sequencing literature or writing, would be effective.

Turning to a standards-based approach, the first step the teacher would take is to start with the standards. ELA standards are grouped by strand, and these strands often include reading literary texts, reading informational texts, writing, speaking and listening, language instruction (including grammar), and, depending on the grade level, additional standards concerning research methods. In considering a logical sequencing of these standards, teachers face much the same problem as exists with sequencing the content. However, important to the task is the desire to present students with a logical sequence of increasingly challenging standards.

In the traditional approach, the teacher selects one of the larger content groups to drive the curriculum sequence. This is, in the case of this eighth-grade teacher, either literature (reading) or writing. Either will work. In the two previously mentioned descriptions, she chose literature as the "spine" around which the sequence of all content revolved. A teacher approaching the problem of sequencing in her own classroom might do much the same thing with the standards. She will choose one strand of standards to sequence for the year and align the other strands to it. For the purposes of this example, the teacher chooses reading.

There are two major reading strands in ELA: (1) reading of literature and (2) reading of informational text. This represents two choices: the teacher can (1) sequence the strands or (2) combine them. For example, consider the following two typical third-grade state standards for ELA—the first for literary texts and the second for informational texts—noting that they are exactly the same.

1. Ask and answer questions to demonstrate understanding of a text, referring explicitly to the text as the basis for the answers.

2. Ask and answer questions to demonstrate understanding of a text, referring explicitly to the text as the basis for the answers.

Although the teacher can apply the standards to different content, she knows the similarities within the standards far outweigh the differences. So, it is likely she would choose to work on both those strands simultaneously across the entire year. From the sequence of those standards, the teacher can connect writing standards, speaking and listening, language, and the rest to the reading strand. For example, as students build their knowledge and skills in reading texts, both literary and informational, teachers can infuse the development of writing, vocabulary, and grammar, as well as speaking and listening skills, within the activities and assessments for the development of reading skills. This means that, in the previous example involving similar literary reading and informational reading standards, the teacher would likely introduce both types of texts at the same time, working on the common reading skills with both. Thus, reading "drives" the curriculum sequence, but no standards are eliminated.

This now establishes the general sequence of the standards across the school year. Next, the teacher looks at what the standards ask of the teacher and of the student, and she looks for a more specific sequence that allows organization of the content. A review of the reading standards indicates that students will work over an extended period of time on reading and interpreting literary and informational texts. Students will work on the skills all year long even though they are challenging and involve a large amount of content knowledge. This means that the traditional sequence of literature—from less challenging to more challenging, from short story to poetry, or from informational text to persuasive passages—would serve the development of the knowledge and skills that the priority standards in reading require.

The specifics of this example are not that important. The more important issue is the analytical approach to developing the learning that the teacher engages to create the sequence of standards. The particular sequence of standards will vary depending on the content area. Some content areas, such as the ELA example, feature standards that are large and apply throughout the entire school year. Other content areas have standards that are more sequential. In this case, one standard is the basis of another, and instructors need to teach them in that sequence. Here there will be many more standards for the year, but only a few that will be in operation at any given time. When students reach proficiency on a certain standard, the teacher removes it from instruction and replaces it with the next standard in the sequence.

It is at this point that experience teaching the class (or grade level) is invaluable. A knowledge of the students involved in the class or grade level and the challenge the standards represent will allow an experienced teacher to accurately judge the proper sequence. Some schools, departments, or districts already provide a pacing guide or scope and sequence. Such a document may or may not be useful in planning for standards-based instruction. If it was developed with a traditional, content-driven approach, it may not help. Consider that any such document should serve the students' needs, not the other way around. The teacher may need to revise any documents that do not approach sequencing of instruction from a standards-based approach before the teacher can use them for planning standards-based instruction.

Once the sequencing process is complete, the teacher has a general plan for the year. The next step is to look at specific units of study and plan how to share this journey with the students.

Creating the Unit Plan

When designing a unit plan, teachers must provide students with a series of scaffolded learning opportunities based on the proficiency scale's learning progression. Understanding that progression is key to creating an effective unit plan. Also essential to the unit design is a focus on priority standards. The priority standard and its associated proficiency scale provide both the teacher and his or her students with the sequence of learning that will guide student growth.

Early in the unit, the focus should be on establishing a solid foundation of the prerequisite knowledge and skills for the priority standard. Focus will then shift to moving past those basics, identifying learning targets that represent the steps in achieving proficiency on the priority standard. At some point in the unit, the teacher will present students with the opportunity to operate both at and beyond the standard. The proficiency scale clearly presents this progression of learning. Obviously, instruction and learning activities will be different at higher and higher levels of the proficiency scale. Students require more direct instruction as they deal with basic knowledge and skills, and they can handle more independent learning opportunities as they achieve and exceed proficiency.

Moving students to and beyond the standard is an important consideration when planning a unit. In a traditional system, teachers facing large amounts of content often feel bound by having to move forward to "cover the content" or "make it through the textbook." In a standards-based system, where the focus moves from covering content to developing student knowledge and abilities as the standards guide, the teacher's task is to help every student reach proficiency on every priority standard. Teachers must find *how* every student can reach proficiency on the priority standards. By carefully selecting priority standards and spending the instructional time to help students reach proficiency and beyond, teachers will provide their students with a deep understanding of the important material. Some content will have to go to make room for this kind of instruction, but the result will be deeper-thinking students who appreciate what they have learned.

Types of Lessons

In order to link the proficiency scale with requisite instructional strategies to operationalize this learning progression, it is useful to identify several different types of lessons students will experience throughout the unit. Marzano's (2017) *The New Art and Science of Teaching* is the basis of the descriptions of lesson types here. Marzano (2017) identifies four types of lessons and associated activities.

1. **Direct instruction (DI) lessons:** When students experience new content, teachers often use instructional strategies that they might describe as direct instruction. In direct instruction lessons, teachers will do many of the things good teachers have been doing for years when they share new content with their students: they identify the important information, chunk the content, provide opportunities for students to process that content, and process the information. Teachers are often in front of the class and leading students through the content by directly presenting it in a direct instruction lesson.

2. **Practicing and deepening (PD) lessons:** Once students have a good grasp on the new content, teachers ask them to engage in activities that deepen their understanding and abilities with that content. Instructional strategies in practicing and deepening lessons are different than when introducing new content and asking students to engage in high-level critical thinking. A few examples include examining similarities and differences, examining errors in reasoning, or using structured practice sessions.

3. **Knowledge application (KA) lessons:** Lessons at this level require students to apply their deep understanding of the knowledge or skills that the priority standard requires in ways that direct instruction lessons or practicing and deepening lessons aren't normally asking. At this level, the teacher's role shifts to facilitator of the learning, and students often work independently on activities such as problem solving, creating and defending claims, investigating, conducting experimental inquiry, and the like.

4. **Strategies that appear in all (All) lessons:** Teachers use some important instructional strategies at every level of instruction. These include strategies such as previewing, highlighting critical information, reviewing, revising knowledge, reflecting on learning, using purposeful homework, elaborating on information, and organizing students to interact. While these strategies may be less likely to define a particular type of lesson in the sequence of developing understanding and ability in the standards, they will be present in the plan.

Figure 1.4 links Marzano's (2017) four types of lessons with the levels of a proficiency scale.

Proficiency Scale Level		Type of Lesson
4	In addition to exhibiting level 3 performance, in-depth inferences and applications that go *beyond* what was taught in class	Knowledge application lessons
3	No major errors or omissions regarding any of the information, processes (*simple or complex*) that were explicitly taught, or all of these	Direct instruction lessons and practicing and deepening lessons
2	No major errors or omissions regarding the *simpler* details and processes *but* major errors or omissions regarding the more complex ideas and processes	Direct instruction lessons
1	With help, a partial knowledge of some of the simpler and complex details and processes	
0	Even with help, no understanding or skill demonstrated	

Source: Marzano, 2017.

Figure 1.4: Lesson types and the proficiency scale.

Although there are exceptions to the relationship this chart depicts, direct instruction lessons, dealing as they do with new content, will occur most often when teachers are dealing with score 2.0 content, and with the initial instruction to score 3.0 content. Once students arrive at score 3.0, teachers move quickly away from direct instruction lessons to practicing and deepening lessons, since these lessons advance the level of rigorous understanding students have of the knowledge and skills that the standards require. Finally, although teachers don't share content labeled as score 4.0 (by definition, score 4.0 has students operating beyond what is taught in class), students have multiple opportunities to demonstrate ability at score 4.0 by experiencing knowledge application lessons, featuring instructional activities that are often student-driven and that require students to apply their deep understanding of score 3.0 content in unique circumstances they have not encountered before.

Sequence of Lessons in the Unit

In linking the proficiency scale to a unit plan, teachers will sequence the type of lessons and their associated content to gradually move students along the learning progression depicted in the proficiency scale. Early on in the unit, students will need work at level 2.0 on the proficiency scale in order to understand and process new information. Eventually, the teacher moves them to level 3.0 activities and offers the opportunity for them to work beyond level 3.0. This provides a logical sequence of activities connected to the learning progression found in the proficiency scale, and that means students are working toward, and possibly beyond, proficiency on a priority standard. Consider the eighth-grade ELA teacher who is working with a standard on identifying theme or central idea of a literary or informational text. One important task for the teacher to consider as she begins the process of creating a unit plan for a priority standard is to consider what proficiency means for the standard. After some thought, the teacher may produce—or have given to her—a proficiency scale for this standard as follows (figure 1.5).

Grade 8 ELA Topic: Theme and Central Idea	
Score 4.0	In addition to score 3.0 performance, the student will make in-depth inferences and applications that go beyond what was taught in class.
Score 3.0	The student will: • Analyze the development of theme or central idea over the course of a grade-level-appropriate text, including its relationship to characters, setting, plot, and supporting details (RL.8.2, RI.8.2) • Provide an objective summary of a grade-level-appropriate text (RL.8.2, RI.8.2)
Score 2.0	The student will recognize or recall specific vocabulary, such as *analyze, central idea, character, development, objective, plot, relationship, setting, summarize, summary, supporting detail, text, theme.* The student will perform basic processes such as: • Determine a theme or central idea of a grade-level-appropriate text (RL.8.2, RI.8.2) • Summarize a grade-level-appropriate text using a teacher-provided graphic organizer (RL.8.2, RI.8.2)

Source: Adapted from Marzano, Yanoski, Hoegh, & Simms, 2013, p. 89.
Source for standards: Adapted from National Governors Association Center for Best Practices & Council of Chief State School Officers (NGA & CCSSO), 2010a.

Figure 1.5: Eighth-grade ELA proficiency scale.

In the case of figure 1.5, the standard falls at score 3.0 and requires students to be proficient in two tasks: (1) analyzing a grade-level-appropriate text for theme or central idea using specific criteria, and (2) objectively summarizing a grade-level-appropriate text. There are two separate learning targets for the score 3.0 performance on this standard. In order for students to achieve proficiency on this standard, they must be able to do both tasks competently and consistently. It is likely that teachers will instruct to both learning targets in a unit on this standard, though there might be instances where they would not teach these two learning targets simultaneously. So, one consideration in designing the unit is sequencing the learning targets. Identifying the learning targets, and their sequence for instruction, is an important first step before teachers can consider the sequence of lessons that they will teach.

Further, teachers should consider the relationship between score 2.0 performance and score 3.0 performance. Score 3.0 contains two learning targets; there are three additional learning targets at score 2.0. The three additional targets are the following.

1. Student will recognize or recall specific vocabulary such as *analyze, central idea, character, development, objective, plot, relationship, setting, summarize, summary, supporting detail, text,* and *theme.*

2. Student will perform basic processes such as determining a theme or central idea of a grade-level-appropriate text (RL.8.2, RI.8.2; NGA & CCSSO, 2010a).

3. Student will perform basic processes such as summarizing a grade-level-appropriate text using a teacher-provided graphic organizer (RL.8.2, RI.8.2; NGA & CCSSO, 2010a).

The vocabulary learning target is a vital first step to score 3.0 performance. These are important terms for students to understand if they are to analyze the development of theme or central idea. The relationship between the score 2.0 learning target on summarizing a text and the score 3.0 target on the same topic is clear. Students will start by learning to summarize a text using a teacher-provided graphic organizer and then proceed to independence in performing this process.

The relationship between the learning targets regarding theme or central idea analysis at the 2.0 and the 3.0 scores is somewhat less clear. At score 2.0 the learning target requires students to *determine* theme or central idea for a grade-level-appropriate text, whereas at score 3.0 students must *analyze* theme or central idea in a grade-level-appropriate text. Consider the difference between the act of determining and the act of analyzing. Objectively, these verbs present different processes, but an important consideration is what is different *for the student*. In other words, what is going on inside the student's mind at score 2.0, and how is it different at score 3.0? In *determining* theme or central idea, students apply a process that one can define in a series of steps. Certainly, students will need to look at important elements of a text, including characterization, plot element sequence, setting, and specific details, but the mental process consists of applying a series of clearly defined steps in order to simply determine theme or central idea. *Analysis* implies a higher level of critical thinking. In this case, the student may rely on a learned process but must think through a broader set of evidence, some of which may appear to conflict with other evidence, looking for and determining the effect of patterns across an entire text. Further, although each learning target applies to a *grade-level-appropriate* text, at score 2.0 it is likely students would receive shorter, less-challenging passages of text as they learn to determine theme or central idea. At score 3.0, students might be engaging with longer texts, perhaps full-length short stories or poems, where they must engage with much more complex evidence, and potentially multiple and even conflicting themes. Thus, in truly analyzing for theme or central idea, the student's mental process represents a much more strenuous engagement with the text and its evidence.

A further consideration is what student performance at score 4.0 would resemble. As previously stated, students are not actually taught content that represents score 4.0 but receive opportunities to perform at score 4.0. An example follows, but at this stage consider that a student working on this standard would most likely exceed proficiency only on the learning target regarding analysis for theme or central idea. The other learning target—summarizing a grade-level-appropriate text—is inherently limited in scope, and the student's mental state would be approximately the same as he or she summarizes any grade-level-appropriate text. It is possible to exceed proficiency by applying summary to a beyond-grade-appropriate text. But consider how a student might exceed proficiency on the learning target involving analysis of theme or central idea.

Students performing at score 4.0 will demonstrate "in-depth inferences and applications that go beyond what was taught in class." Score 4.0 performance becomes a measure of the qualitative difference between analysis at the 3.0 score and analysis at 4.0. At score 4.0, the student might apply analysis of additional literary devices, perhaps ones that are beyond grade level (for example, tone). Or the student might do an exceptionally perceptive analysis of the grade-appropriate text, in which the reasoning is much deeper and more accurate than performance at score 3.0. It is also possible that the student can apply analysis to challenging texts beyond grade level.

Taking into account the analysis of the proficiency scale for eighth-grade ELA theme and central idea, the following unit plan (figure 1.6) is one way in which a teacher can sequence the types of lessons to provide learning opportunities for her students. Where applicable, we indicate in this figure which activities are connected to specific levels of the proficiency scale. Some aspects of the plan (for example, sharing the scale and learning target) are not specific to a scale level so no level is indicated. (For additional information, see *The New Art and Science of Teaching*, Marzano, 2017.)

Key:	
LG = Activities to provide and communicate clear learning goals	KA = Knowledge application lessons
	All = Strategies used in all lessons
DI = Direct instruction lessons	Assessment = Assessment activities
PD = Practicing and deepening lessons	
Day One	Present and explain the proficiency scale for the priority standard for the unit. (LG)
	Introduce the topic of theme or central idea—lecture and discussion. (LG)
	Provide direct instruction on key vocabulary terms—*analyze, central idea, character, development, objective, plot, relationship, setting, summarize, summary, supporting detail, text, theme.* (Score 2.0—DI)
	Homework—read short excerpts and identify characters, setting, and plot elements. (Score 2.0—All)
Day Two	Brief review of content covered day one. (Score 2.0—All)
	Review and correct homework activity. (Score 2.0—All)
	Model procedure for summarizing a grade-level-appropriate text using a teacher-provided graphic organizer. (Score 2.0—DI)
	Engage students in practice regarding summarizing a text using a graphic organizer. (Score 3.0—PD)
	Homework—independent practice using a graphic organizer to summarize a grade-level-appropriate text. (Score 2.0—All)

Figure 1.6: Sample unit plan for theme and central idea.   Continued →

Key:	
LG = Activities to provide and communicate clear learning goals	KA = Knowledge application lessons
	All = Strategies used in all lessons
DI = Direct instruction lessons	Assessment = Assessment activities
PD = Practicing and deepening lessons	

Day Three	Remind students about learning goals and proficiency scale. (LG)
	Review and correct homework activity. (Score 2.0—All)
	Model procedure for analyzing theme or central idea in a text. (Score 3.0—PD)
	Engage students in practice regarding identifying theme or central idea using elements such as character development, setting, and plot. (Score 3.0—PD)
	Homework—independent practice summarizing text independently and identifying theme or central idea using character development, setting, and plot elements. (Score 3.0—All)
Day Four	Have students assess their current level of knowledge relative to the proficiency scale. (Assessment)
	Conduct comparison activity on topic and theme. (Score 3.0—PD)
	Homework—review for assessment on theme or central idea. (Score 3.0—All)
Day Five	Remind students about learning goals and proficiency scale. (LG)
	Administer test on theme or central idea. (Assessment)
	Introduce concept of development of theme across a complex text. (Score 3.0—DI)
	Model procedure for analyzing development of theme across a complex text. (Score 3.0—PD)
	Engage students in guided practice on tracing development of theme across a complex grade-level-appropriate text. (Score 3.0—PD)
	Homework is independent practice in analyzing development of theme in a complex text. (Score 3.0—All)
Day Six	Remind students about learning goals and proficiency scale. (LG)
	Review homework assignment on analyzing development of theme in a complex text. (Score 3.0—PD)
	Have students self-assess their current level of knowledge relative to the proficiency scale. (Assessment)
	Conduct error analysis involving typical mistakes made when tracing development of theme in a complex text. (Score 3.0—PD)
Day Seven	Administer test on analyzing development of theme or central idea in a complex grade-level-appropriate text. (Assessment)
	Organize students into groups for analysis of a challenging text for theme or central idea. (Score 4.0—KA)

Day Eight	Student groups select text for analysis, tracing the development of theme or central idea through literary elements including character, setting, plot elements, tone, and additional literary devices. (Score 4.0—KA)
	Student groups read and analyze text, comparing their findings and formulating a claim for theme or central idea. (Score 4.0—KA)
Day Nine	Students continue to read and analyze a complex text for evidence supporting their claim for theme or central idea. (Score 4.0—KA)
Day Ten	Individual students plan and write their arguments supporting their claim for theme or central idea in the examined text. These written arguments are sent for teacher review. (Assessment)
	Student groups meet together to synthesize the findings of each student member's findings. (Score 4.0—KA)
	Student groups plan presentations on theme or central idea in their complex texts. (Score 4.0—KA)
Day Eleven	Student groups present their analysis of texts for theme or central idea. (Score 4.0—KA)
	Conduct a whole-class review with feedback on student group presentations of their claims and defense of their claims regarding theme or central idea development in a complex text. (Assessment)

Source: Adapted from Marzano, 2017, pp. 107–108.

A quick review of this unit plan reveals the lesson sequence's logic. Starting with the score 2.0 content from the proficiency scale, vocabulary terms and prerequisite knowledge and processes such as the ability to summarize the text with a teacher-provided graphic organizer and a process for determining theme or central idea, students progress through the content of score 3.0 and receive the opportunity to perform at score 4.0. The speed at which this progress occurs is less important than the sequence. Perhaps this same unit might occur across twenty instructional days instead of eleven.

Also note that the unit plan does not identify specific content to teach. It will become important to align specific passages of text with each instructional activity and homework assignment, but the content will merely support the unit plan's sequence of instruction to the standard and its learning targets.

Further, note how often assessment, in various forms, takes place. In an eleven-day period, five assessments occur. Some of these assessments are informal student self-assessments, but these give important instructional feedback to the teacher and the students, indicating how the students perceive their own progress toward the learning targets. The formal assessments provide the teacher with the opportunity to use the information from these assessments formatively, deciding whether to continue with the unit plan as initially sketched, or to make adjustments, returning to content students have yet to master, reteaching as needed and so forth.

In summary, we define the process for sequencing a unit plan in this manner as a series of four steps.

1. The teacher identifies the priority standard and associated scale that he or she will teach during the unit of instruction. (This can be more than one priority standard. For purposes of explaining the process, we limit the example here to a single standard, but with multiple standards the process is the same. Instruction to each standard is integrated throughout the unit plan.)

2. The teacher reviews the proficiency scale to be clear about the learning progression from score 2.0 to score 3.0 and on to score 4.0. The teacher identifies the number of learning targets at each score of the scale.

3. The teacher proceeds to build the unit plan day by day, including:

    ▶ Adapting the sequence of lessons to scaffold learning through the scale's scores

    ▶ Making frequent reference (often) to the learning goals and the proficiency scale

    ▶ Discussing how homework will play a role in supporting the unit's learning progression

    ▶ Giving assessments often enough for students and teachers to use the results of the assessments formatively

4. The teacher reviews the unit plan and makes adjustments.

It is also true that the teacher should ask students to progress as rapidly as possible through the scaffolded learning. Expect faster progress than has been seen in a traditional approach in the past, since the focus of instruction is narrower with standards-based learning. At the same time, as always, the teacher should be sure to provide sufficient learning experiences for students to make progress before he or she asks students to perform at the next score level of the learning target. Developing a "feel" for the pace of instruction takes time. Teachers should make informed decisions early on but be ready to do some adjusting in the first few units taught in this manner.

For an example of how the same process can be applied at the elementary level, please see appendix B (page 145). This appendix illustrates the creation of a unit plan for a second-grade mathematics unit.

The logical and straightforward process for creating unit plans presented thus far in the chapter can be applied to multiple different teaching frameworks and templates that teachers may already be using in their classrooms. The following section presents an example of adapting the previously presented standards-based method of unit design to a sample planning template.

Using a Planning Template

A well-organized template that captures the unit designer's thinking as the unit plan is developed can aid not only the teacher doing the design but also teachers who may review or use the unit plan later. The example that follows (see figure 1.7) is a modification of a template developed by Uinta County School District #1 in Wyoming. This template uses the four questions central to the PLC process (DuFour & Marzano, 2011, pp. 22–23) as a starting point, with the addition of an important question for planning: "How will teachers facilitate the learning?" In following the sequence of these PLC questions, the teacher addresses each aspect of curriculum and instruction necessary to meet the needs of all students.

Grade:		
Unit:		
PLC Question One: What do we want all students to know and be able to do?		
Grade-Level Priority Standards: • • •		
Supporting Standards: • • •		
Essential Questions: Questions to probe for deeper thinking and promote the development of critical thinking and higher-order capabilities, problem solving, and understanding complex systems. • • •		
Learning Progressions		
Previous Grade-Level Standards: • • •	**Grade-Level Standards:** • • •	**Next Grade-Level Standards:** • • •

Figure 1.7: Sample planning template.

Continued →

Student-Friendly Learning Targets
Standard: •   **Potential Success Criteria:**   •   •   •
Essential Vocabulary
Key Academic Vocabulary: Refer to resource.   **Scaffolded (Review) Academic Vocabulary:** Refer to score 2.0 vocabulary from scales.

PLC Question Two: How will we know when students have learned?
Assessment and Evidence

State-Required Assessments:	District Essential Assessments:	Supporting Evidence:
• •	• •	• •

Priority Standard Proficiency Scale	
Score	**Standard**
Score 4.0	In addition to score 3.0 performance, the student will make in-depth inferences and applications that go beyond what was taught in class.
	3.5: No major errors or omissions regarding 3.0 content and partial knowledge of the 4.0 content.
Score 3.0	The student will:
	2.5: No major errors or omissions regarding 2.0 content and partial knowledge of the 3.0 content.
Score 2.0	The student will: Academic vocabulary: Prerequisite knowledge:
	1.5: No major errors or omissions regarding 1.0 content and partial knowledge of the 2.0 content.
Score 1.0	With help, the student will achieve partial success at score 2.0 content and score 3.0 content.

Planning Question: How will teachers facilitate the learning?	
Key Curriculum Resources and Instructional Strategies	**Supporting Resources and Instructional Strategies**
	Additional lessons needed for standards: Digital tools:
PLC Question Three: What will we do when students have not learned?	
Interventions	
Tier 3—Intensive:	Tier 2—Supplemental:
PLC Question Four: What will we do when students have learned?	
Enrichment	
Additional Questions	
How will we increase our instructional competence?	
How will we coordinate our efforts as a collaborative team?	

A quick review of this template will demonstrate how the information developed through the four-step process mentioned previously (page 22) can be used to complete the template. PLC questions one and two are directed toward identifying the specific state (or provincial) standards that teachers will address in the unit and determining the assessment methods that will measure student progress toward, and past, proficiency. In the case of this template, state- and district-level assessments are cited; the teacher could also substitute specific assessments their students will take or simply use classroom teacher-designed or common assessments. The template then includes a sample proficiency scale, which teachers can use as the basis for the answer to the planning question. In answering this question, the teacher would include the sequencing of lessons as outlined in the unit plan example mentioned previously (see figure 1.6, page 19), using the proficiency scale as the basis for that design. Question three requires teachers to consider how they will respond when student learning has stalled, and question four considers what will happen to students who have reached proficiency while the unit is still underway—this is essentially level 4.0 on the standard.

In using a version of this template, we can include the planning from our previously provided example of the eighth-grade ELA teacher designing a unit on theme or central idea (see figure 1.6, page 19). The completed template might look like the example in figure 1.8.

Grade: 8

Unit: Theme and Central Idea

PLC Question One: What do we want all students to know and be able to do?

Grade-Level Priority Standards:

The student will:

- Analyze the development of theme or central idea over the course of a grade-level-appropriate text, including its relationship to characters, setting, plot, and supporting details (RL.8.2, RI.8.2).
- Provide an objective summary of a grade-level-appropriate text (RL.8.2, RI.8.2).

Supporting Standards:

-

Essential Questions:

- How do authors create messages in their texts?

Learning Progressions		
Previous Grade-Level Standards:	**Grade-Level Standards:**	**Next Grade-Level Standards:**
- Determine a theme or central idea of a text and analyze its development over the course of the text (RL.7.2). - Provide an objective summary of the text (RL.7.2, RI.7.2). - Determine two or more central ideas in a text and analyze their development over the course of the text (RI.7.2).	- Analyze the development of theme or central idea over the course of a grade-level-appropriate text, including its relationship to characters, setting, plot, and supporting details (RL.8.2, RI.8.2). - Provide an objective summary of a grade-level-appropriate text (RL.8.2, RI.8.2).	- Determine a theme or central idea of a text and analyze in detail its development over the course of the text, including how it emerges and is shaped and refined by specific details (RL.9–10.2, RI.9–10.2). - Provide an objective summary of the text (RL.9–10.2, RI.9–10.2).

Student-Friendly Learning Targets

Standard:

- On my own, I can identify the important features of a text and explain how they create a theme or central idea.

- On my own, I can summarize a grade-level text.

Potential Success Criteria:

- Student creates a summary of a grade-level-appropriate text and then goes on to identify important rhetorical features and use that information to accurately identify theme or central idea.

Essential Vocabulary

Key Academic Vocabulary:

analyze, central idea, theme

Scaffolded (Review) Academic Vocabulary:

character, development, objective, plot, relationship, setting, summarize, summary, supporting detail, text

PLC Question Two: How will we know when students have learned?

Assessment and Evidence		
State-Required Assessments: • •	**District Essential Assessments:** • •	**Supporting Evidence:** • Successful completion of teacher-designed test on theme and central idea. • Successful completion of a paper or project in which student completes all aspects of analysis of theme or central idea independently.

Priority Standard Proficiency Scale	
Score	**Standard**
Score 4.0	In addition to score 3.0 performance, the student will make in-depth inferences and applications that go beyond what was taught in class.
	3.5: No major errors or omissions regarding 3.0 content and partial knowledge of the 4.0 content.

Figure 1.8: Sample completed unit design template.   Continued →

Score	Standard
Score 3.0	The student will:
	2.5: No major errors or omissions regarding 2.0 content and partial knowledge of the 3.0 content.
Score 2.0	The student will: Academic vocabulary: Prerequisite knowledge:
	1.5: No major errors or omissions regarding 1.0 content and partial knowledge of the 2.0 content.
Score 1.0	With help, the student will achieve partial success at score 2.0 content and score 3.0 content.

Planning Question: How will teachers facilitate the learning?	
Key Curriculum Resources and Instructional Strategies	**Supporting Resources and Instructional Strategies**
Day One: Present and explain the proficiency scale for the priority standard for the unit. (LG) Introduce the topic of theme or central idea—lecture and discussion. (LG) Provide direct instruction on key vocabulary terms—*analyze, central idea, character, development, objective, plot, relationship, setting, summarize, summary, supporting detail, text, theme.* (Score 2.0—DI) Homework—read short excerpts and identify characters, setting, and plot elements. (Score 2.0—All)	Additional lessons needed for standards: Digital tools:
Day Two: Brief review of content covered day 1. (Score 2.0—All) Review and correct homework activity. (Score 2.0—All) Model procedure for summarizing a grade-level-appropriate text using a teacher-provided graphic organizer (Score 2.0—DI) Engage students in practice regarding summarizing a text using a graphic organizer. (Score 3.0—PD) Homework—independent practice using a graphic organizer to summarize a grade-level-appropriate text. (Score 2.0—All)	

Day Three: Remind students about learning goals and proficiency scale. (LG) Review and correct homework activity. (Score 2.0—All) Model procedure for analyzing theme or central idea in a text. (Score 3.0—PD) Engage students in practice regarding identifying theme or central idea using elements such as character development, setting, and plot. (Score 3.0—PD) Homework—independent practice summarizing text independently and identifying theme or central idea using character development, setting, and plot elements. (Score 3.0—All)	
Day Four: Have students assess their current level of knowledge relative to the proficiency scale. (Assessment) Conduct comparison activity on topic and theme. (Score 3.0—PD) Homework—review for assessment on theme or central idea. (Score 3.0—All)	
Day Five: Remind students about learning goals and proficiency scale. (LG) Administer test on theme or central idea. (Assessment) Introduce concept of development of theme across a complex text. (Score 3.0—DI) Model procedure for analyzing development of theme across a complex text. (Score 3.0—P&D) Engage students in guided practice on tracing development of theme across a complex grade-level-appropriate text. (Score 3.0—PD) Homework is independent practice in analyzing development of theme in a complex text. (Score 3.0—All)	
Day Six: Remind students about learning goals and proficiency scale. (LG) Review homework assignment on analyzing development of theme in a complex text. (Score 3.0—PD) Have students self-assess their current level of knowledge relative to the proficiency scale. (Assessment) Conduct an error analysis involving typical mistakes made when tracing development of theme in a complex text. (Score 3.0—PD)	

Key Curriculum Resources and Instructional Strategies	Supporting Resources and Instructional Strategies
Day Seven: Administer test on analyzing development of theme or central idea in a complex grade-level-appropriate text. (Assessment) Organize students into groups for analysis of a challenging text for theme or central idea. (Score 4.0—KA)	
Day Eight: Student groups select text for analysis, tracing the development of theme or central idea through literary elements including character, setting, plot elements, tone, and additional literary devices. (Score 4.0—KA) Student groups read and analyze text, comparing their findings and formulating a claim for theme or central idea. (Score 4.0—KA)	
Day Nine: Students continue to read and analyze a complex text for evidence supporting their claim for theme or central idea. (Score 4.0—KA)	
Day Ten: Individual students plan and write their arguments supporting their claim for theme or central idea in the examined text. These written arguments are sent for teacher review. (Assessment) Student groups meet together to synthesize the findings of each student member's findings. (Score 4.0—KA) Student groups plan presentations on theme or central idea in their complex texts. (Score 4.0—KA)	
Day Eleven: Student groups present their analysis of texts for theme or central idea. (Score 4.0—KA) Conduct a whole-class review with feedback on student group presentations of their claims and defense of their claims regarding theme or central idea development in a complex text. (Assessment)	

Key:	
LG = Activities to provide and communicate clear learning goals	KA = Knowledge application lessons
DI = Direct instruction lessons	All = Strategies used in all lessons
PD = Practicing and deepening lessons	Assessment = Assessment activities

PLC Question Three: What will we do when students have not learned?	
Interventions	
Tier 3—Intensive:	**Tier 2—Supplemental:**
One-to-one instruction to develop analytical skills either during differentiated instruction on days seven through eleven or in pull-out program.	Targeted additional instruction and practice throughout the unit.
PLC Question Four: What will we do when students have learned?	
Enrichment	
See activity days seven through eleven.	
Additional Questions	
How will we increase our instructional competence?	
How will we coordinate our efforts as a collaborative team?	

Source: © 2017 by Uinta County School District #1. Used with permission.
Source for standards: Adapted from National Governors Association Center for Best Practices & Council of Chief State School Officers (NGA & CCSSO), 2010a.

In adapting the planning work from our example to this template, for PLC question one, "What do we want all students to know and be able to do?" we have included the priority standard in two learning targets. It is possible that we could have added some supporting standards, though in this case we have chosen not to. Supporting standards receive instruction but would likely not be assessed, though their role in any given unit is an important consideration, and the template can prompt the teacher to think through that issue. We have recorded the previous and the next grade-level standards, looking at the logical progression of skills from year to year. In this case, the previous and next grade-level standards are very similar, but in many cases the standards are substantially different and teachers should consider the learning progression on the specific skills and content in the standard. Next, we have translated each of the learning targets into language the teacher can use in the classroom with students and identified one potential way in which a student might demonstrate proficiency on these targets. Finally, we have broken down the level 2.0 content on academic vocabulary into two categories: (1) *key* vocabulary terms which might be defined as those that are absolutely essential to proficiency on the standard, and (2) *scaffolded* academic vocabulary, those important terms that are covered and learned by students at level 2.0 but are often a review of terms learned in prior units or years of instruction.

For PLC question two, "How will we know when students have learned?" the template directs the teacher to identify possible sources of assessment data. In the case of our example, the assessments will be teacher-created, but it is equally possible that there may be state- or district-level assessments that will provide data on student performance on this priority standard. The template requires the teacher to consider each of those possibilities.

Next, we include the proficiency scale we have been working from to design the learning for this unit. The next question, "How will teachers facilitate the learning?" allows the teacher to input the specific daily lesson activities developed when creating the unit plan, and here we capture both the learning progression inspired by the proficiency scale as well as the sequence of assessments that permit the teacher to make formative judgments about student progress as the learning develops. In the process of adding those specific activities, the template asks the teacher to consider supporting resources, like the textbook or close reading passages, that the teacher may commonly use each year in instruction. Additionally, the teacher considers any digital tools that may be appropriate for this unit. In our example, there are no additional resources.

The last two questions—"What will we do when students have not learned?" and "What will we do when students have learned?"—are vital considerations when creating a unit. We have built in opportunities for intervention on the unit plan we created, so these find their place in the template under the question about what to do when students have not learned. (Additional discussion of intervention methods can be found in the following section, Differentiation With Response to Intervention.) We have also considered learning opportunities for those students who move beyond proficiency in the form of the knowledge application lesson from days seven through eleven, and this provides an effective answer to the question of what to do with students who already have learned the material and are at or above the standard.

Thus, whether teachers plan with a template or simply by applying the four-step process outlined in this chapter, planning in standards-based learning involves considering each student's learning needs for the unit ahead. Unlike traditional planning, standards-based learning starts with the standard as the centerpiece of the learning, and from there the teacher aligns the content to the learning progression on the standard.

Differentiating With Response to Intervention

Even in the planning stage, teachers need to consider what to do when students do not progress to proficiency in the expected manner, and when some students are ready to do higher-level work while others are still working on the basics at score 2.0 and lower. Response to intervention (RTI) provides a framework for considering these possibilities. Thus, a quick review of the basics of RTI is in order.

RTI is available for *all* students, not just those who are in need of intervention. Although the RTI model provides intervention options at three different tiers, and teachers must access these, as needed, to do everything possible to help struggling students, it also suggests the need for intervention for those students who are ready to move beyond the limitations of proficiency on the standard, as represented by score 3.0 on the proficiency scale. For those students, true differentiation in the classroom may offer a solution.

To review the basics of RTI, consider the three tiers of intervention. Austin Buffum, Mike Mattos, and Janet Malone (2018) state:

> The pyramid is commonly separated into tiers: Tier 1 represents core instruction, Tier 2 represents supplemental interventions, and Tier 3 represents intensive student supports. The pyramid is wide at the bottom to represent the instruction that all students receive. As students demonstrate the need for additional support, they receive increasingly more targeted and intensive help. Because timely supplemental interventions should address most student needs when they are first emerging, fewer students fall significantly below grade level and require the intensive services Tier 3 offers, creating the tapered shape of a pyramid. (p. 2)

The tiers are traditionally represented in the form of a pyramid, as shown in figure 1.9.

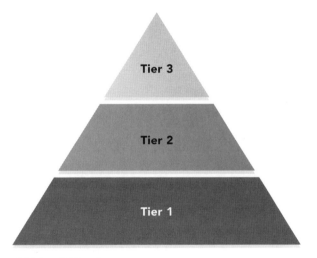

Source: Buffum, Mattos, & Malone, 2018, p. 2.

Figure 1.9: Traditional RTI pyramid.

Buffum et al. (2018) continue:

> With this approach, the school begins the intervention process assuming that every student is capable of learning at high levels, regardless of his or her home environment, ethnicity, or native language. Because every student does not learn the same way or at the same speed, or enter school with the same prior access to learning, the school builds tiers of additional support to ensure every student's success. The school does not view these tiers as a pathway to traditional special education but instead as an ongoing process to dig deeper into students' individual needs. (p. 19)

Moving students to a score 4.0 activity approximately halfway through the unit raises the concern for those students who have yet to master score 2.0 or score 3.0 content, or both. It will often be true that not all students in the class will be ready to take on high-level work at the same time. Teachers should include those students who can benefit from participating in the knowledge application activity. Knowledge application activities are student centered; the teacher's role shifts toward facilitation. This means that while the teacher introduces the activity and monitors student progress as the activity goes forward, for much of the time during which the knowledge application activity is proceeding, the teacher is available for one-to-one remedial instruction with students who require it. The classroom becomes truly differentiated for a short period of time, providing a range of activities to meet students' individual needs.

Summary

Teachers shifting to standards-based instruction from a traditional approach will find significant adjustments when planning instruction. Planning will begin with an under-standing of the priority standards and will focus largely at the unit level. The proficiency scale provides a learning progression on the standards that will allow students to gradually progress to or beyond proficiency on the priority standards. Whether one uses *The New Art and Science of Teaching* framework or another instructional planning framework or template, sequencing lessons, activities, and assessments using a proficiency scale will provide students with a steady challenge and consistent feedback on their progress toward proficiency.

Now that teachers have planned for instruction, the next chapter will focus on instruction using proficiency scales.

Instructing With Proficiency Scales

Once teachers have created a strong unit plan around one or several priority standards, instruction can begin, again based around proficiency scales. The unit plan provides general guidance, but teachers now need to connect instructional strategies with the current level of student performance.

A teacher familiar with instructing in a traditional manner may find the instruction process this chapter describes rather foreign. In the sense that the central focus of instruction—the standard, rather than the content—is very different, this may be so. Teachers switching to standards-based learning may feel overwhelmed at first and unsure whether they will be able to make such a profound change to their instructional practice.

The reality is that once teachers change to standards-based instruction, they find that *what* they teach does not change very much. Even *how* they teach what they teach doesn't change very much. But how the teacher *thinks* about what he or she teaches changes substantially. In working with veteran teachers who have made the shift to standards-based learning, we often hear them report that standards-based learning provides a clarity to what occurs in the classroom they had not seen before—a clarity they are eager to share with their students. Everything in the classroom, from planning to instruction to assessment and feedback, centers on student growth on the priority standards, and the conventional content is still there as the vehicle for that growth. After an initial transition period, most teachers discover a comfort level with standards-based learning, and even prefer it to traditional methods.

This chapter will discuss several sequential aspects of instruction with proficiency scales. First, it will introduce the pros and cons of preassessments, or benchmark assessments. Then, it will discuss how to introduce the proficiency scale to students, begin content instruction, assist students with developing proficiency, and move past proficiency.

Administering the Preassessment

An important first step is to identify where students reside on the proficiency scale at the start of instruction through the use of a *preassessment*. Although student performance will likely be poor since no instruction has taken place, both teacher and students must be aware of the starting point for learning. It is also likely that students will know some of the preassessment information, since students may have background knowledge from previous instruction earlier in the class, or from other classes. Knowing the starting point of each student, teachers can then guide students along the learning progression, with the goal of having every student achieve proficiency on the priority standards by the end of the learning period. Not all may get there, but it will certainly be the goal, one that teachers will continuously share with students.

Although we recommend preassessments at the start of instruction of each priority standard, there are pros and cons for the use of preassessments. The most important pros of preassessments include gaining clear understanding of the starting point of each student and understanding the background knowledge and abilities of the class as a whole. The cons consist primarily of the instructional time lost when giving these assessments and the effect that an initial low score may have on students. The lost instructional time is minimal and offset by a clear understanding of the direct needs of the students in starting the learning progress, which means the teacher can be much more efficient in designing learning experiences that immediately move students along that progression. If students are properly instructed in how to interpret low initial scores, they can be encouraged that the score will quickly change. Focusing less on the score and more on the future growth is key. Teachers might encourage students by saying, "It's no problem that you are at a 1.0 score in the proficiency scale at the start, as long as we're working on 2.0 and then 3.0!" Saying this often enough will create an atmosphere of growth in the classroom and focus students less on their current grade and more on the future.

In creating a focus on growth, teachers can consider the work of Carol S. Dweck in identifying student mindsets around academic work. In *Mindset: The New Psychology of Success*, Dweck (2006) delineates the traits of what she calls the *fixed* and the *growth* mindsets and indicates that students' ideas about their potential for academic growth can be guided with only a few shifts in the way in which student performance is discussed in the classroom. For example, the addition of a single word—*yet*—in a teacher's language can show students that they have the potential to grow in their abilities. Additionally, sufficient repetition, accompanied by many of the techniques explained later in this book, can help students see that working hard at goals and expecting growth will genuinely pay off. When the student complains "I can't do this," the teacher can respond by simply saying, "You can't do this—*yet*. But you will. Keep trying."

If score 3.0 represents proficiency on the priority standard, instruction generally begins at score 2.0. Score 2.0 represents the prerequisite knowledge and skills students require for success at 3.0, so starting there assures that students have the requisite background knowledge in place. The benchmark assessment may indicate some deep holes in students' knowledge, and that may require stepping back even farther, effectively starting at 1.0. But in most cases, teachers begin instruction at 2.0.

After initially administering a preassessment and collecting baseline data on students' topic knowledge, teachers should introduce the proficiency scale (or scales) they will be using throughout the unit.

Introducing the Proficiency Scale

As the sample unit plans in chapter 1 (figure 1.6, page 19) and appendix B (figure B.2, page 146) indicated, teachers should begin instruction with teaching the proficiency scale to students. Eventually students will understand the role of the proficiency scale, but in the first few units of the year, teachers often need to remind them of the proficiency scale's importance. Students should understand that proficiency scales:

- Set the unit learning goal (usually proficiency on the standard at score 3.0)

- Help them identify their current performance in relation to the overall learning goal

- Identify the next steps in the journey toward proficiency on the learning goal

- Describe the learning progression they will undertake, and thus provide clarity as they set and work toward accomplishing their own personal goals on the priority standard

Teachers often wonder whether a benchmark test is a good idea, since it often indicates that students have a long journey ahead of them in reaching proficiency. As teachers talk with their students about the learning journey ahead, it will be important to reassure students that it takes time to achieve the goal. No one should expect students to be proficient at the start of the unit. In that sense, it is perfectly fine for students to be at score 1.0 or 2.0 on the proficiency scale, as long as they are working on getting to 3.0. Teachers must continually reassure students that learning takes time, and steady but often slow progress is the goal.

During this step, teachers must then perform three tasks vital to the success of standards-based learning in their classroom: (1) converting the proficiency scale to student-friendly language, (2) sharing the proficiency scale with students, and (3) helping students set personal goals based on the proficiency scale.

Converting the Proficiency Scale

Since it is vital that students understand what they need to know and be able to do to succeed in class, the proficiency scales that teachers use to plan instruction and to judge student growth are likely inappropriate for sharing with students. Thus, teachers must first convert scales into student-friendly language, both in vocabulary that is developmentally appropriate and in a format that helps students focus on their growth. At lower grade levels, using *I can* statements is particularly effective. Although it requires enormous amounts of instructional time, having students participate in rewriting the standards into language they understand is highly effective in helping them focus on the learning progression ahead. While it is unlikely teachers would devote instructional time to having students rewrite every scale in this way, having students participate in the process on one or two key standards can have big payoffs in terms of student buy-in.

There is also an important advantage of discussing with students the proficiency scale as a learning progression. Such a scale will encourage students on their journey up the scale; they will understand that they are making progress even though they may not have reached proficiency yet. This is essential in developing student self-efficacy and helping them understand that they are building abilities gradually. It also reinforces a growth mindset (Dweck, 2006), helping students understand that the work they are doing is resulting in academic growth.

Sharing the Proficiency Scale With Students

In sharing the proficiency scale with students for the first time, teachers should communicate that the learning goal provides clarity on the various learning targets in the scale, particularly with regard to proficiency on the standard. Students must understand what they need to know and be able to do when they have reached proficiency on the standard. Although instructional time is always at a premium, spending sufficient time early on in the unit to ensure clarity on the standard will be worth it in the long run. Because students understand exactly what proficiency on the learning target will be, and what steps they will take on the journey to proficiency, they understand the relevance of much of the work they will undertake. Further, they will be well placed to identify and appreciate their own growth on the learning progression to proficiency.

Providing students with sample student work at each level of the scale is very helpful in establishing clarity. These examples can be work from previous years, even if that work was not completed in a standards-based classroom. Teachers can assess whether the sample student work aligns to the priority standard and at which score of the proficiency scale. In future years, as students work in a standards-based classroom, teachers will have access to more examples at each level of the scale. Of course, teachers must obtain permission for the use of this work from students and their parents, and the original students' names should be removed from the work.

The proficiency scale itself should be prominently visible within the classroom. There are a number of ways to do this, depending on the resources available to the teacher. If the classroom has a projector and screen connected to the teacher's computer, the teacher can easily and frequently project the proficiency scale at the front of the room. He or she could also display an enlarged form of the proficiency scale on a bulletin board on the classroom wall or draw up a modified scale on a large poster sheet and tack it on a wall for easy reference. Remember that it is up to the teacher to continually reference the proficiency scale. If the teacher values and continually emphasizes the proficiency scale, students will begin to do so as well. The effect of doing so may be quite surprising; in our experience of teaching with standards-based learning, we have found that students will shift their focus away from the grade they are receiving and toward the learning progression of the proficiency scale, noting often that their own learning, rather than the reward of a grade, is their focus.

One effective way to always have a proficiency scale available in the classroom is to use a generic scale (see figure 2.1) that teachers can apply to any activity or assignment in which students are engaged. It is important to note that a generic scale does not take the place of a proficiency scale specific to the learning goal for a particular lesson or unit. Students must always understand the specific learning goals teachers are asking them to master. But within the context of the larger learning target, a generic scale can be useful for quick, on-the-fly instructional feedback. (For additional information on student-friendly generic proficiency scales, see Marzano, 2010.)

How Proficient Am I?	
4	I can do this! I can teach this! I can apply what I learned! (Application)
3	I can do this by myself! I mastered this! (Target)
2	I can do the easy stuff! The hard stuff is still too hard for me! (Prerequisite and vocabulary)
1	When I have help I can do some of the easy and hard stuff. (With help)
0	Even when someone helps me, I can't do it yet. (Not yet)

Source: Marzano, 2010.

Figure 2.1: Student-friendly generic proficiency scale.

*Visit **MarzanoResources.com/reproducibles** for a free reproducible version of this figure.*

Helping Students Set Personal Goals

Once students are clear regarding the learning they will undertake, they are ready to do some personal goal setting. This is an essential step in the standards-based classroom. (See chapter 3 on page 47 for greater detail.) Student goal setting and tracking of progress on personal goals have been associated with as much as a 32 percentile point gain in student achievement (Marzano, 2010). For this reason, teachers should not skip this step. However, students who are not used to setting and tracking goals may be skeptical of the practice. In order to access the high levels of performance indicated by research in this area (Marzano, 2010), teachers need to be sure to advocate for the practice on a regular basis. That means planning for the instructional time it will take to set goals, process feedback on the goals, discuss with students their progress on the goals, and celebrate success as students see gains toward their goals. Teachers should also reference the proficiency scales often during instruction as a method of reinforcing the importance of the learning progression during instruction, assessment, and feedback.

After students set personal goals, they must have regular access to them. If students have academic notebooks, they can keep goal sheets there and update them regularly. Recommendations for goal setting and tracking of student progress with goal sheets in described in detail in chapter 3 (page 47). If more appropriate, teachers can organize folders in the classroom for students to keep their goal-tracking forms and evidence of progress on the goals in the form of assessments and assignments, with scores providing feedback on the progress students are making toward their goals. Having student-set goals, and identifying and tracking progress toward those goals, means that both student and teacher have the information available to make regular check-ins about progress meaningful.

Teachers often wonder about the logistics of having multiple priority standards and their associated proficiency scales in operation at the same time. While it is certainly possible for teachers to instruct to and assess many standards at the same time, students may find it challenging to maintain their focus on many goals at once. One way to address this problem is to guide students to focus on and set goals for only one or two priority standards per unit. Teachers should decide on one or two standards as the most important for the current unit, and particularly ones that will continue to be important for the units that follow.

Once teachers successfully convert and share their proficiency scales with students and help them create personal goals, they are ready to begin content instruction.

Beginning Content Instruction

After introducing the proficiency scale and the learning goals to students, the teacher should now begin content instruction. Although the unit plan provides the overall sequence of lessons, teachers must now assign specific instructional strategies to each portion of the unit plan. Teachers can find several instructional strategies aligned with direct instruction lessons, as well as with the other levels of the proficiency scale, in *The New Art and Science of Teaching* (Marzano, 2017) and *The Marzano Compendium of Instructional Strategies* (Marzano, 2016). Teachers should refer to these texts for further information on specific instructional strategies.

Importantly, although the teaching strategies used in standards-based learning are often traditional in nature (for example, choosing to use cooperative learning activities in a practicing and deepening lesson), teachers may find that their understanding of *why* one chooses to use these traditional strategies is now informed by their own deep understanding of the learning progression as identified in the proficiency scale. In other words, while a teacher might have used cooperative learning before, in standards-based learning the same teacher chooses to use that strategy at a particular place in the learning progression, while working on level 3.0, because of the effects of the strategy—deepening the students' understanding and bringing it to a more rigorous level as required by the priority standard. This is one way in which standards-based learning provides clarity about instruction often unseen in traditional instruction.

Using the sample eighth-grade ELA unit on theme or central idea from chapter 1 (see figure 1.6, page 19), teachers will notice that day one of the sample unit plan is as follows.

- Present and explain the proficiency scale for the priority standard for the unit.

- Introduce the topic of theme or central idea—lecture and discussion. (LG)

- Provide direct instruction on key vocabulary terms—*analyze, central idea, character, development, objective, plot, relationship, setting, summarize, supporting detail, theme*. (DI)

- Homework—read short excerpts and identify characters, setting, and plot elements. (All)

In presenting the learning goal and proficiency scale to the students (see Introducing the Proficiency Scale, page 37), the teacher will accomplish the first two bullets in this plan. The next step is vocabulary instruction on key terms, a direct instruction (DI) lesson at score 2.0 on the proficiency scale.

When considering the key vocabulary terms for eighth-grade students listed in figure 1.6, it is clear that few of these terms will be new to most students. The concepts of *plot, setting, character*, and perhaps even *central idea* or *theme*, are ideas they have already worked with in previous years. So, the goal of the vocabulary instruction is twofold: (1) to reacquaint students with their prior knowledge and (2) to refine that knowledge in the direction the teacher wishes to apply these terms in the unit at hand. Additionally, there are two terms that are likely new to students, at least in the context of reading texts: *objective* and *supporting detail*. For these terms, the teacher can still access some background knowledge but should focus strongly on the use of the term in an analytical way as applied to texts. These considerations are important to identify as he or she selects the instructional strategy for vocabulary instruction.

After the first few days of the unit plan, it is reasonable to conduct some informal (instructional feedback from students about their own perceptions of their progress on the learning target) and perhaps a formal (pencil and paper, or other teacher-created) formative assessment of student learning on vocabulary terms. Although the teacher will cover terms on day one of the unit plan, students are not ready for assessment at that point. They will need to apply the terms on successive days as they begin working on summarizing a grade-appropriate text on day two and take on the first stages of analyzing texts for theme and central idea on day three. At the same time, teachers will be making informal judgments of students' knowledge of vocabulary during instruction on days two through four. If necessary, the teacher can clarify vocabulary terms during that instruction, and can give an individual, vocabulary-based assessment on day four if the teacher deems it necessary.

A strategy Marzano (2017) suggests in developing students' content knowledge and skills during direct instruction lessons is the K-W-L strategy (Ogle, 1986). In the three columns of the K-W-L strategy, students record:

- **K**—What they *know* in the first column to establish background knowledge

- **W**—What they *want to learn* in the second column to create questions about the learning they will engage in having understood their own background knowledge

- **L**—What they *learned* in the third column to provide an opportunity for students to process what they learned within the context of their recorded background knowledge and the questions they created

Students can use the K-W-L chart as the lesson moves forward to record their progress on understanding the terms within the context of the unit.

The next step of the lesson is to address the specific new understanding and applications of the terms—the *W* column. In providing clarity about the use of and difference between two very similar terms, such as *central idea* and *theme*, the teacher might use the Concept Attainment strategy (Marzano, 2016). In using this strategy, the teacher asks students to identify and compare and contrast examples and nonexamples of each concept. Gradually, students will refine their specific understanding of the terms and record them in the *L* column of the K-W-L chart. At the end of the lesson, students record questions they may still need to understand in the *W* column.

At the end of such a direct instruction lesson, students will have an emerging understanding of the vocabulary terms for the unit, but their understanding will need practical application. A useful way to end the lesson would be to provide sample short, grade-level passages that ask students to apply the terms of *analysis, identifying characters, setting, plot elements, supporting details, objectives, central idea,* and *theme*. In the case of setting, teachers might ask students to identify a setting using the term's definition as it applies to a short literary passage. In the case of *theme* or *central idea*, the teacher might ask students if a particular statement of theme or central idea meets the term's definition. (The teacher would avoid asking students to identify the theme of the text themselves, as this would represent a separate learning target from the vocabulary at score 2.0.) After some guided practice in this manner, students are then ready to apply their understanding in independent practice for homework.

All assessments in a standards-based learning classroom are aligned to the priority standards as described in chapter 1 (page 7), so the teacher may examine the data obtained, representing student progress on that standard, as the students begin and progress through the unit. Obviously, these data affect teacher decisions throughout the unit of instruction. Early in the unit, assessments will likely show that students require more direct instruction and practice on prerequisite knowledge before they can move up the learning progression on the grade-level standard. If the class as a whole is progressing more slowly than anticipated, the teacher might extend the instructional time for the unit or change the instructional focus and strategies for the beginning of the unit. Essentially, assessment assists teachers in their judgments of student and class proficiency toward the learning goals. The following section discusses teacher strategies for a class on its way to developing proficiency.

Developing Proficiency

As the unit plan moves forward, students will proceed to practicing and deepening (PD) lessons. Here, the instructional strategies are more rigorous and deepen students' understanding of the content and procedures necessary for proficiency on the standard. These lessons might include engaging students in structured practice sessions, asking students to examine similarities and differences, and so on (Marzano, 2017). As mentioned in the previous section, Beginning Content Instruction (page 40), the teacher will continue to provide assessment opportunities and analyze the results to see how students are progressing. In the example regarding the eighth-grade scale on theme and central idea (figure 1.6, page 19), it is reasonable that the assessment on day five would address scores 2.0 and 3.0 by requiring students to define vocabulary terms (score 2.0), summarize a grade-level text (score 3.0), and analyze a grade-level text for central idea or theme (score 3.0). At that point in the unit plan, students will have learned how to summarize a grade-appropriate text without teacher assistance in the form of a graphic organizer, and teachers can now assess this skill at the score 3.0 level. Further, they have begun to work at the score 3.0 level on the target of analyzing a grade-level text for central idea or theme.

In the case of some students near proficiency and others in need of major amounts of remediation before they can work on proficiency for the learning goal, teachers may have difficulty truly differentiating instruction this soon in the unit. Although differentiation is always challenging, the use of a proficiency scale with articulated and leveled learning targets, as well as an aligned assessment, can make the task easier. Assessments aligned with the proficiency scales clearly and easily pinpoint any areas of deficiency and identify specific students in need of remediation, students who are at or beyond grade level on the standard, and students who are ready to begin grade-level instruction to the standard. As with using a proficiency scale with response to intervention (RTI; see page 32), the scale identifies not only the students with unique needs for a particular standard but also the specific nature of those instructional needs, so teachers can tailor their instruction to meet those needs.

Differentiating instruction can, at times, be overwhelming to a classroom teacher tasked with finding how every student in his or her classroom can learn. Standards-based learning provides some options that can help with this workload. Because student needs are individually identified as previously described, and interventions can be tailored to those specific needs, student progress may be accomplished more quickly. It is also possible, in some cases, for multiple classroom teachers who teach the same content to share the differentiation workload. For example, during a common intervention period, where two teachers are teaching the same priority standard and proficiency scale, one teacher might take on the differentiated instruction for students needing intervention at level 1.0 on the scale, while the other might work with the students needing help at level 2.0.

As students work toward proficiency, teachers need to be aware of the moments when progress stalls, or possibly recedes. There are multiple opportunities for assessment in the unit plan, whether in the form of formal assessments of all class members, individual student assessments, or informal instructional feedback from students about their perceptions of their own progress on the learning goal. Knowing when to change the unit plan based on formative assessment data is both an art and a science, but teachers should be prepared to review assessment information often—at least every other class—to make formative decisions about their students' progress.

The assessment data may suggest that, as a class, students have not made sufficient progress to be successful on a higher-level activity at this point in the unit. If, as a class, student average performance on the score 3.0 learning targets hovers closer to 2.0 than 3.0, then the teacher may decide that it is time for some reteaching, remediation, or additional direct instruction or practicing and deepening that provides more opportunities for more students to get closer to score 3.0 on the learning progression before attempting knowledge application activities. Again, this must be the judgment of the teacher as to the best use of the instructional time for the most students. However, while some students may continue to struggle to reach proficiency, the teacher must also consider the instructional needs of students who are near, at, or beyond proficiency and are ready for a higher challenge.

In spite of our best efforts, there may be some students who do not make much progress at all on the proficiency scale. As the rest of the class works its way toward, and in some cases beyond, proficiency, there are some students who, for various reasons, cannot exceed score 1.0 performance. In addressing these students' needs, an important issue is timing. Informal and formal assessment data, as well as teacher anecdotal data, will suggest early on in the unit that these students are in need of additional help. It is at this point, early on, that teachers must consider intervening.

Yet, there are students who, despite everything teachers try, simply are unable to score above 1.0. In this case, one strategy is to set up some incrementally less-challenging mileposts for the student, so he or she can see some progress even though this progress may not be at the stages that the proficiency scale defines. The teacher will still use the grade-level proficiency scale for reporting overall student performance on the standard but will provide moments for a student who is struggling when, by celebrating incremental success, the student is encouraged to continue working hard. Still, progress may be substantially behind his or her grade-level peers.

In situations such as these, teachers must remember the purpose of standards-based learning, and the reporting of student progress in a standards-based environment. One important reason for adopting standards-based learning is to report grades that show what students know and are able to do. The aim is to provide feedback to students and parents about students' real progress on the standards. In the case where a student, despite trying everything tried, is still at score 1.0, the teacher will report that score as evidence of the current level of student learning on that standard. Of course, in identifying the student as a candidate for RTI and adopting those procedures, it will be important to involve the parents at every tier of intervention, so the reporting of a score of 1.0 on a progress report will not come as a surprise to either the students or their parents. But in reporting that score, the teacher is accurately reporting what the student knows and is able to do on that standard. Let us be honest—such conversations are not easy. But with standards-based learning, with assessments aligned to show student progress on the priority standards, teachers have the aligned data to present to the student and his or her parents or guardians to demonstrate what has been done and the progress, such as it is, that the student has made.

Eventually, when most students are at or near proficiency, the opportunity to move into knowledge application (KA) lessons provides many students with opportunities for true independence on the standard. The following section will discuss this topic.

Moving Past Proficiency

Once students achieve proficiency, they have reached a very important point in the unit with regard to making formative judgments about their further progress. The rest of the unit is designed to offer students the opportunity to work at, or above, score 3.0 performance on the proficiency scale. The teacher must decide whether the students, as a class, are ready for that next learning experience.

It is at this point that the *art* of teaching is important. Teachers must use their own best judgment about whether the class as a whole moves on to the next level or not. While it is rare that an entire class reaches one level of the proficiency scale at the same time, it will often be true that most of the class will. Waiting until everyone is at the same point means that many students already proficient will *wait* for other students to catch up. Moving the class too quickly to the higher levels of the scale means that many students will struggle with the new work. The teacher must use his or her best judgment on when to move, and it helps to keep in mind the opportunities for differentiating instruction described earlier as this decision is made. Do the assessment data suggest that students would benefit from more independent work? For example, data may indicate steady progress on the learning target on analyzing a grade-level text for theme or central idea. In terms of the learning target on summarizing a text, assessments might show that students are proficient, and the additional learning activities above score 3.0 will provide them with opportunities to apply that skill. They are also proficient on the vocabulary terms (score 2.0) and will be able to apply that knowledge in the days ahead. Such data would indicate a class is likely ready to move into activities beyond proficiency. Not every student will achieve a score 4.0 performance, but many will benefit from participating in such high-level activities as they continue to achieve proficiency on the standard.

Returning to the eighth-grade ELA class in our example, the teacher now moves students into the KA activity. Students will complete an individual written argument for day ten of the unit, and the teacher will assess those documents for the learning target on analyzing theme or central idea on a grade-level text. This will provide additional data on the progress of that learning target. The final assessment is the whole-class review of the presentations of all the students' analyses of texts. Teachers can also ask individual students to record their own comments from the whole-class review to create an individual evaluation, so there will be an additional score contributing to the assessment of that target.

An important consideration in making judgments about moving to advanced content is that although assessment data are important and useful, *they are only one part of the decision*. The teacher knows his or her students well and is with them every class. Teaching is both an art and a science (Marzano, 2017). The aligned assessment data provide the concrete information about student progress that lets teachers make scientific judgments about student progress, but teachers bring the art of personal judgment to those same decisions.

However, it is often the case that there are a few students who may not be ready to move past proficiency. It might also be true that there are one or two additional students who might also, in the teacher's judgment, be overly challenged by a high-level activity at this point. What is in these students' best interest as the unit proceeds? It might be the case that most of the class takes on the knowledge application activity while the teacher works one-to-one or in small groups with students who are still far from proficient, helping them to make faster gains on these learning targets than they have been able to make as members of the larger class. The learning progression of the proficiency scale and the design of the unit builds in some flexibility with regard to differentiation that teachers can access at this point in the unit.

Instruction in a standards-based learning classroom may often look just like instruction in a traditional classroom, but the teacher is now equipped with an understanding of the progression of learning in the curriculum and aligned assessment data that allows him or her to make informed judgments about the progress of his or her students in ways not possible in a traditional classroom. Although the methods described in this chapter may appear to be an enormous change in the way teachers instruct, in reality teachers often find the change is minimal. Their understanding is clarified in standards-based learning, but their instructional methods are often similar to what they have done before.

Summary

In this chapter, we have examined how a teacher delivers planned instruction in a standards-based classroom. Starting with a proficiency scale aligned to a priority standard, the teacher can align instruction to the particular level of the scale represented by the students' current progress on the learning progression of the scale. Instruction is thus aligned more closely to student needs.

In the next chapter, we discuss how to work with students to establish and track progress on students' personal learning targets.

3

Setting Goals and Tracking Progress

Goal setting is an integral part of a standards-based learning environment because it helps focus students on individual needs related to specific learning targets, and because the most important and influential instructional decisions are often made by learners themselves (Stiggins, 2008). Goal setting and tracking progress go hand-in-hand. As students set goals, they track progress about those standards-based learning targets. In turn, tracking progress provides students with information regarding their initial goals, and often will assist them in modifying the goal or creating a new one.

Edwin A. Locke and Gary P. Latham (1990) surmised that goal setting helps students learn in four distinct ways: (1) goals focus students' attention on both the task and target of learning, (2) goals stimulate effort, (3) goals increase students' persistence, and (4) goals improve students' capacity and desire to adopt new learning strategies. When teachers focus students on goal setting in standards-based learning environments, "students develop into more confident and competent learners, they become motivated (energized) to learn, increasingly able to persist during demanding tasks and to regulate their own effort and actions" (Moss & Brookhart, 2009). Additionally, Hanson (2016) suggested teachers reflect about goal setting with students on a continual basis. It should be a cyclical process that compels teachers to designate time in the classroom for students to reflect about, discuss, and share the ways they are establishing and reaching their standards-based goals.

The potential for these positive outcomes make it imperative to address goal setting as part of the standards-based learning process. Goal setting is not a new practice. Teachers have often asked students to set goals around behaviors and content for years. Yet, goal setting in a standards-based learning environment is imperative. Marzano, (2017) identified academic goal setting as one of the strategies for motivating and inspiring students. Hattie (2009) reiterated this in his research synthesis by stating, "Motivation is highest when students are competent, have sufficient autonomy, set worthwile goals, get feedback, and are affirmed by others" (p. 48). According to Andrew J. Martin, Herb Marsh, and Raymond L. Debus (2001), "When students feel they have control over the outcome of any given situation, such as academic achievement, they seem to handle disappointment, demands, and fear of failure more productively" (as cited in Chapman & Vagle, 2011).

This chapter will discuss several aspects of goal setting, including when to set goals in a standards-based learning classroom, types of goals, and strategies for teaching goal setting. It will then discuss ways teachers and students may track progress toward goals, either individually or classwide, and celebrate that success.

Setting Goals

Goal setting is a metacognitive process that motivates students and helps them modify their learning behaviors. Setting goals helps students learn and achieve to higher levels, as goal setting and increased student achievement coexist (Zimmerman & Martinez-Pons, 1988). Yet there are some distinct approaches that must occur for teachers to make the benefits of goal setting a reality. Teachers must consider when to set goals in a standards-based classroom, types of goals, and strategies to teach and model the goal-setting process to realize the greatest benefits for students.

When to Set Goals

Goal setting must be a continuous process of learning how to learn. Connie M. Moss and Susan M. Brookhart (2009) reiterated, "Teachers often think of goal setting as a periodic event rather than a continuous part of the learning process" (p. 63). To change this, schedule time for students to reflect on their goals on an ongoing basis. Begin by carving out time once to twice per week for goal setting. Adjust that timeframe based on your students' ages. Some younger students (grades K–3) may need to review a goal daily for a while, whereas older students (grades 4–12) can wait a bit longer. Some teachers use Reflective Fridays to review the week's work, accomplishments, learning, and goals. Whichever schedule you choose, ensure that the event occurs regularly.

Types of Goals

The type of goal students set has the potential to affect learning outcomes. Some goals intend for students to compare themselves to a set of criteria, while others may be more of a comparison to other students. When students have a *comparative orientation* approach to goal setting, their goals primarily focus on grades. This tends to encourage students to compare themselves with others in a normative manner (Ames, 1992; Pope, 2010). For example, a student using a comparative orientation might say, "I will increase my grade from a B to an A, like some of my friends," or, "I want to raise my proficiency scale score from a 2.0 to a 3.0 so I can put my sticker on the 3.0 chart with other kids." Such types of comparison-orientated goals are generally associated with increased negative student outcomes, like a decrease in student motivation and corresponding achievement (Meece, Anderman, & Anderman, 2006). As Caitlin C. Farrell, Julie A. Marsh, and Melanie Bertrand (2015) noted, "Although some students may be motivated by performance [comparison] orientation, others may balk at difficult tasks and give up when faced with difficulty" (p. 16). In contrast, a *mastery orientation* approach to goal setting occurs when students focus on setting goals that will develop and improve their personal knowledge, skills, and competence through self-regulation, effort, and autonomy (Farrell et al., 2015). The self-efficacy attribution of growth mindsets, rather than fixed ones (Dweck, 2010), plays into this concept of mastery orientation. When students have a mindset of growth, they think they can control what happens to them, they have increased motivation and achievement. On the other hand, students who have a fixed mindset base their achievement on a perception of innate abilities and intelligence—being smart or not.

Teachers can encourage their students to set mastery-orientated goals in a number of ways. Table 3.1 depicts key differences in teacher behaviors that may encourage either comparison or mastery orientation goals in their classrooms.

Table 3.1: Comparison and Mastery Orientations

Teacher Behaviors That Reflect a Comparison Orientation	Teacher Behaviors That Reflect a Mastery Orientation
The teacher: • Publicly shares group-level data or individual results in the belief that social comparison motivates students • Uses extrinsic rewards like prizes and parties when students move to a certain proficiency status • Provides limited opportunities for student involvement; simply shares results • Provides little guidance about what students should study or revisit	The teacher: • Helps students identify weaknesses, ways to address gaps in learning, and so on • Focuses on growth-related feedback by showing a clear relationship between effort and outcomes • Encourages students to chart their results • Shares individual-level results privately with students • Focuses attention on how students perform in relation to their past performances and standards • Sometimes uses intangible rewards like praise and discussion of results toward progress • Involves students in analysis, goal setting, and follow-up • Uses whole-group or individual interventions, and multiple approaches for reteaching

Source: Adapted from Farrell, Marsh, & Bertrand, 2015.

Farrell et al. (2015) found that some teachers have mixed-goal behaviors, essentially leading to a hybrid of comparison- and mastery-oriented goals in their students. These teachers might use mastery orientation during personalized goal setting but also provide comparison charts for students to see their progress compared to others. While in some settings this may be appropriate, teachers in a standards-based learning classroom should primarily ensure their students' goal-setting practices are mastery oriented in nature. Students need to see their personal results as they progress along a proficiency scale, and teachers should expect them to use their individual results for progress tracking and goal setting. As the classroom culture becomes such that students can see themselves and others as simply different, not as *smart* or *dumb*, comparison graphs may be helpful, although we would suggest that teachers keep any identifiable student data (names, for example) anonymous. However, the majority of students will make best progress when their goals are mastery oriented.

In addition to the teacher behaviors described in table 3.1 (page 49), another way to encourage more mastery-oriented goals is to use reflective prompts. Reflective prompts provide students with incomplete statements that the students must complete. These prompts require students to think critically about their own learning. Sample reflective prompts include the following.

- Prompts about preferences:
    - ▸ "The most interesting thing about _____ was . . ."
    - ▸ "I prefer to work by myself on activities that . . ."
    - ▸ "I like working with others when . . ."
- Prompts about learning style and strategies:
    - ▸ "If I can, I try to avoid activities that . . ."
    - ▸ "I find it easiest to understand when . . ."
    - ▸ "When I don't understand something, I . . ."
- Prompts about strengths:
    - ▸ "I'm getting much better at . . ."
    - ▸ "One good question I asked (or thought of) today was . . ."
    - ▸ "One of the things I do best is . . ."
- Prompts for improvement:
    - ▸ "I'm still not sure how to . . ."
    - ▸ "I need to get help with . . ."
    - ▸ "The part I find the most difficult was . . ."

Another technique involves using reflective questions with students. Some sample reflective questions teachers might use include:

- "What have you learned?"
- "What did you find easy about learning to . . . ?"
- "How would you do things differently next time?"

- "What did you find difficult while you were learning to . . . ?"
- "What helped you when _____ got tricky?"
- "How could you recognize or refine your (feedback) data practices to reflect more mastery?"

For instance, a student may discuss how not knowing the academic vocabulary from a proficiency scale was the cause of a lower performance rating (2.0). He or she would then make sure to practice the vocabulary and use it in conversations and assignments to ensure mastery of it. As a result, a mastery-oriented goal helped a student recognize an area of needed improvement from the proficiency scale, create a plan of action, and then see how it would help him or her on the assessment of that particular standard.

Some teachers find that they can best stimulate critical thinking when reflection questions align with goal setting in a student reflection form. Figure 3.1 is an example of a form containing reflective questions and some potential student responses. This reflective-processing form links feedback with reflective questions and goal setting. Students discuss what they did well and why, and consider next steps for future work. Teachers who encourage student reflection by using these prompts and questions help students practice reflection, consider appropriate actions, and employ those actions for increased achievement. In a standards-based classroom, specific knowledge and skills necessary are described within a proficiency scale. This helps students better understand the components of a particular standard and also monitor how they are doing against that specified knowledge and skills set. Therefore, it eliminates guessing what is important to know and be able to do.

As you reflect about what you wrote and the expectations, what did you do well? How do you know? What is your evidence?
I did well. One thing was to include a lot of info that connects to the expectations. It states that we needed logical information, and to make my project logical, I included opinions along with the backing quotes from the text. That is evidence.
What are the next steps that you will focus on in your next project? Why? Remember to connect your ideas back to the expectations.
I worked hard, and still have some things I would do differently. For example, I would have added more points of view, like what the boys thought of the BTS group, that would have made my write-up more interesting and informative. I think I will take a bit more time to see that I have a piece of text evidence for each point I made. I will do that next time.

Figure 3.1: Sample student responses to reflective questions.

Reflective questions seek specific responses to teacher-posed questions. They should be related to a component on the proficiency scale; thus, teachers may want to use the proficiency scale's bulleted items to create reflective questions. The same is true with reflective prompts, although a prompt differs from a question in format. It uses a sentence starter to prompt the student's thinking, seeking completion of the prompt in order to create a completed sentence about the proficiency scale content. Prompts and questions may be used at any point in the learning, though it should be noted that prompts tend to be a bit more summative in nature, typically asking students to reflect on something already done. Reflective questions, on the other hand, may be used as feedback by teachers or peers to stimulate more action during the learning process.

An additional reflection form can be seen in figure 3.2. This form, from a freshman English literature and composition course, provides students with connections between the prioritized standard and reflective questions.

Writing Personal Learning Targets

When you set out to be successful in this class, it is important to know what success looks like. We have priority standards in this class, but in this activity, we will try to make them useful to you each day in class.

Let's start with this question: What kind of things do successful English students know and do?

Now, let's put the preceding answers into categories. List the categories we come up with in class in the following space:

Categories

For each category, we will have a priority standard. We will look at each standard, eventually. Today, we will look at the reading one.

> Textual analysis: The learner understands and applies the techniques of textual analysis to a wide variety of literary genres.

After reading this standard, list questions you have and the answers we come up with in class:

Now, write the standard in your own words. Hint: *You can make this personal by making "I can" statements. Be ready because we may share our standards aloud!*

Be sure you clearly understand what you have written!

After all, you're the one who will work on this.

Now, let's set a goal! Goals have the following elements:

- A clear level of performance that you think you can reach
- A time period that will allow you to accomplish your goal
- A sense that once you've reached your goal, it isn't just a "one and done"—you can keep right on doing the performance!
- It must match the standard for which you are writing the goal (check it against the standard you wrote above)

Source: Adapted from Flygare, 2012.

Figure 3.2: Sample goal-setting form.

*Visit **MarzanoResources.com/reproducibles** for a free reproducible version of this figure.*

After students respond to these types of reflective prompts, they have the basis for setting *new* goals. When students note challenges in response to the prompts, they can turn those challenges into goals. For instance, take Sarah, who wrote a prompt response about what was difficult for her during her long division process. The challenge for her was remembering the last step of bringing the remaining numbers down after subtracting during long division. This now becomes a small goal she sets for herself. Her goal might be completing three new long division problems, remembering to bring the remaining numbers down each time without prompting from her teacher.

Additionally, when students note something about their learning process in response to such types of teacher prompts, that becomes an action step. To continue with the preceding example, Sarah also notices that when she doesn't understand something, she can quietly check with her seat partner. So, she creates two action steps.

1. She circles the part of the process when she brings down the remaining numbers, in order to draw her attention to that part of the process.

2. She quietly checks in with her seat partner to show him or her and to get immediate feedback. After all three problems, she shows her work to her teacher.

Sarah uses a strategy she created (or learned) and pairs that with an additional feedback loop (her partner). By doing so, she can monitor her practice along the way, immediately noting if employing the strategy proves beneficial in changing her practices and improving her success. The hope is that Sarah will continue to use this strategy in the future in a self-directed manner for improving her knowledge of and skills on the standard until she eventually doesn't need this step any longer.

Thomas R. Hoerr (2014) discussed the importance and types of goals teachers may consider for changing their own thinking and behaviors. Grit goals and personal and professional goals are relevant to students and teachers in a standards-based learning classroom. Hoerr (2014) described the *grit goal* as something that individuals may only have a fifty-fifty chance of obtaining. It intends to extend the individual beyond his or her comfort zone, to push individuals (either adults or students) into experimentation. In contrast, a *personal* and *professional goal* is a private type of goal that affects professional performance. It intends to make a difference in both the goal setter's life and work. While teachers may not want to *begin* the goal-setting process with students with these types of far-reaching goals, they may become worthy of consideration as students attain goals they set for themselves and become more sophisticated in the goal-setting process. These types of goals ooze into the realm of life attainment. Robert J. Marzano and Debra J. Pickering (2011) reiterated this point when they stated, "Perhaps at the highest level are goals that address life ambitions" (p. 87).

It is not enough to implicitly use such goal-setting strategies with students. Educators must also teach them more explicitly. In the following section, we discuss specific strategies for teaching goal setting.

Strategies for Teaching Goal Setting

Teachers should use a combination of two approaches to teach goal setting: (1) modeling goal setting and (2) explicitly teaching students goal setting. The following sections discuss these approaches.

Modeling Goal Setting

One of the best ways to encourage students to set goals that will stimulate learning is to let them see you, as a teacher, set and make progress toward goals. Teachers should continually model goal setting and ensure that students see them do it. Students will feel inclined to set goals themselves as they see the growth and successes that stem from setting goals.

Begin with specific goals and strategies that students can meet and understand. For example, a middle school teacher may show students a professional goal he set for increasing engagement in his classes. He may explain that one way in which his end-of-year student survey results suggested he improve is having more engaging, hands-on activities to help students learn. Consequently, his goal is to embed three hands-on activities per week in his lessons. He will not only keep track of these in his lesson-planning template but also ask his students this year to rate him on occasion. His hope is that by increasing hands-on activities, classes are perceived as more engaging and fun and will result in even better student achievement on the standards.

An example of a grit goal may include a secondary teacher who wishes to begin student-led conferencing in her school. She will plan it, inform parents, provide students with practice, and implement it. Afterward, she will obtain feedback from students and parents about their perceptions of using the student-led conferencing model in the future. This is a grit goal because it will take a tremendous amount of individual initiative, and because it requires a philosophical shift in the practices her school is using. This teacher may be the only one holding such conferences, and she may or may not be successful in all aspects of implementing them.

Finally, an elementary health teacher may model a personal goal with his students. During their wellness unit, he explains that his personal goal will be to incorporate meditation into his daily routine as a means for managing stress. He describes the process he will use for meditation, referencing a cell phone app. He aims to practice meditation daily for four weeks and track his progress weekly. He will share the results with his students at the end of four weeks. This personal goal modeling will assist students in recognizing that teachers, too, set personal goals, and it will encourage his students to do the same.

Another way to introduce goal setting via modeling is through accounts of famous individuals setting goals. By selecting an account from a famous individual that students will relate to, teachers encourage their students to emulate the goal-setting behavior. A good example is the following excerpt from business mogul and professional basketball legend Michael Jordan's (1994) *I Can't Accept Not Trying*, which summarized the significance of Jordan's goal-setting process. In his book, Jordan (1994) detailed how he frequently set short-term goals:

> I had always set short-term goals. As I look back, each one of those steps or successes led to the next one. When I got cut from the varsity team as a sophomore in high school, I learned something. I knew I never wanted to feel that bad again. I never wanted to have that taste in my mouth, that hole in my stomach. So I set a goal of becoming a starter on the varsity. That's what I focused on all summer. When I worked on my game, that's what I thought about. When it happened, I sent another goal, a reasonable, manageable goal that I could realistically achieve if I worked hard enough. Each time I visualized where I wanted to be, what kind of player I wanted to become. I guess I approached it with the end in mind. I knew exactly where I wanted to go, and I focused on getting there. As I reached those goals, they built on one another. I gained a little confidence every time I came through. (pp. 2–4)

This excerpt, and other motivational pieces like it, help students see that successful individuals often use the process of goal setting. After sharing such an account, have students pair up and discuss the celebrity's ideas. For example, students might compare or contrast how their goal setting is similar to or different than Jordan's. They might ask, "What did Michael Jordan do when he had a setback? What about when he achieved a goal?" Those types of reflective questions help connect the learning at hand to the larger process of goal setting in life.

In addition to modeling goal setting for students, it is also important to teach them goal-setting skills overtly. We discuss these strategies next.

Explicitly Teaching Student Goal Setting

Students of all ages and all grades learn more when they take ownership of their learning through an effective goal-setting process (Moss & Brookhart, 2009). Bena Kallick and Allison Zmuda (2017) stated:

> Because students may not be accustomed to setting their own goals and determining their own direction for further study, beginning the process can be puzzling. Here, teachers play an important role as guides. They need to help students discover nuggets of gold in the curriculum. They need to offer a balance of guidance without taking over the direction. (p. 31)

Moss and Brookhart (2009) shared that goal setting is more effective when "guided by three core questions for students: Where am I going? Where am I now? What strategy or strategies will help me get to where I need to go?" (p. 61). Clear learning targets and proficiency scales (as discussed in chapter 1, page 7), paired with quality feedback (to be discussed in chapter 6, page 121), answer the first and second questions. Students will gain a substantial level of understanding when they fully understand the levels of the scale. Setting personal goals invests students in the learning progression, and often students report a real desire to engage in the work of the unit of study so they can receive feedback on their personal goals. Elementary students often take to goal setting and tracking as a fun activity that directly involves them. With older students, especially at the secondary level, they may see goal setting and tracking of their progress as not worthy of their time. When this occurs, one strategy is to share the research on goal setting and tracking (see, for example, Lemov, 2010; Marzano, 2009, 2016). Students should understand that the activity has a direct potential payoff for them, personally. Teachers should also enthusiastically support student goal setting and tracking of progress as important tools for student learning. What teachers value, students will value.

Moss and Brookhart's (2009) third question—What strategy or strategies will help me get to where I need to go?—requires more discussion. As one might suspect, high-achieving students tend to self-regulate more automatically. Those who internalize "learning how to learn" boost their achievement by up to 30 percent (Zimmerman, 1998), whereas students who achieve lower often need to learn these skills more directly. Moss and Brookhart (2009) reiterated that point: "High-achieving students know what is important to learn and how to learn it" (p. 61). Goal setting helps those students who achieve lower learn how to learn and energizes their productivity (Locke & Latham, 1990, 2002). This is where teachers must be ready with a plethora of strategies to help students, at varying levels of proficiency, learn and use tactics to support the differentiated learning targets. Effective goal setting cannot be an assumed skill. Rather, teachers need to teach it with the same zest as their content.

To explicitly teach goal setting to students, there are three phases for consideration. They include: (1) setting the goal, (2) setting strategies to obtain the goal, and (3) reviewing and reflecting on the goal regularly (Moss & Brookhart, 2009).

Setting the Goal

First, set the goal (or goals). Instruct students that the initial goal should be specific, short-term, and "just right" in terms of difficulty of challenge and attainment (Pintrich & Schunk, 2002; Stipek, 2002). Goal setting should be personal and focus on obtainable learning targets. Although teachers should ultimately aim for students to transfer short-term goal setting into long-term goals, such as career and schooling aspirations, it is best to keep initial goals related to the learning at hand (Moss & Brookhart, 2009). Using proficiency scales for tracking progress and setting goals ensures the goal is relevant to current learning and keeps students focused. An effective goal is precise and links to the classroom tasks, not to general academic gains. One example of an appropriate goal might be an elementary student who writes, "My goal is to get a 3.0 (proficient) about knowing my multiplication facts." The goal is small in nature, relates to a specific learning target, and ties specifically to the student (reflecting a mastery orientation). A middle school example might be, "My goal is to be consistently proficient in writing a thesis statement." Again, the goal relates to a learning target specific to the individual and small enough to obtain in a relatively short timeframe. Finally, let's look at an option for a high school student: "My goal is to be able to show how two triangles are congruent when corresponding angles and sides are also congruent." Once again, the goal reflects specificity, achievability, and individualization to the student.

One way to conceptualize goals that are just right is through SMART goals (see figure 3.3). The acronym SMART (strategic and specific, measurable, attainable, results oriented, and time bound) has been found in much goal-setting literature (Conzemius & O'Neill, 2013). Giving people specific goals to achieve, rather than vague generalities, best increases their motivation (see Locke & Bryan, 1966; Locke & Latham, 2002). Using a template may assist students in creating their just right (SMART) goals.

SMART Goal Areas	Student Application	Student Evidence and Reflection	Teacher Review and Feedback
Strategic and specific			
Measurable			
Attainable			
Results oriented			
Time bound			

Figure 3.3: SMART goals template.

*Visit **MarzanoResources.com/reproducibles** for a free reproducible version of this figure.*

Students will often connect one part of the 3.0 portion of the proficiency scale to a SMART goal. In some instances, it may be all of the bulleted components of the proficiency scale. This will depend, in part, on the complexity of the standard and the grade level of the student. As an example, consider the SMART goals shown in figure 3.4, which could be used with the eighth-grade proficiency scale on theme and central idea referenced previously in chapter 1 (page 7).

To inspire goal setting, teachers could also encourage students to set nonacademic goals, such as ones for relaxation and enjoyment. National Board Certified Teacher Nancy Barile (2015) mentioned, "One of my students included the goal 'Learn to moonwalk.'" When students create nonacademic goals as well, they will see a transference of the process into everyday life.

Setting Strategies to Obtain the Goal

Next, help students select a strategy to attain the goal (or goals), being mindful that some students may need guidance for this part of the process. Barile (2015) suggested a way to do this may be to have students plan strategically and tactically. The *strategic* part of goal setting, completed when students set their initial goals, pushes students to plan with the bigger, yet specific goal in mind; for example, "Get to proficiency on the next geometry standard," "Write an accurate lab write-up," "Complete the mile run in seven minutes," or "Try out for the one-act play." Now, students must turn to the *tactical* part of an action plan, which asks students to break that big picture into smaller, doable increments. When creating specific action items, teachers should encourage students to use verb-noun structure. Barile (2015) noted:

> Action items must *drive* the student to action—not simply be part of a "to do" list. Each action item should begin with a verb: "Attend every class," "Review notes with study partner before major tests," "Finish homework each night."

If a student's goal is "Get to proficiency on the next geometry standard," his or her action items need to include the steps to achieve that goal: "Complete all my practice homework," "Describe my processes aloud," and "Attend extra help sessions," as an example (Barile, 2015).

Consider having students create action plans (see figure 3.5, page 60) that specify the goal, strategies, time line, and notes to assist students in their goal setting. Be certain students include a time line. Some goals and strategies may be ongoing, while others have specific time allotments. For example, for seniors applying to college, action items with deadlines are critical. Make sure students include time lines when applicable, and encourage them to sync those time lines with their calendars to achieve the best results. (Note: The first two columns will not necessarily be completed every time. Students will more frequently use the final three columns to track their progress.)

Another helpful idea for older students (grades 4–12) is to identify obstacles to success. Identifying obstacles clarifies the action plans and helps students to problem solve as well. Some students will modify their strategies later based on the obstacles they encounter. For instance, a student may identify an obstacle of studying in a quiet place, as her home is too noisy with little brothers and sisters. Therefore, she may consider other locations or times when she can find quiet in her home to better concentrate.

SMART Goal Areas	Student Application	Student Evidence and Reflection	Teacher Review and Feedback
Strategic and specific	Analyze central idea including its relationship to characters, setting, plot, and supporting details.	Place a check mark next to each: the character, setting, plot, and supporting details.	During my teacher-student conference for this unit, I will share my goal and progress with my teacher.
Measurable	Count the number of times I share the central idea by including characters, setting, plot and supporting details.	I had five check marks next to elements of the central idea.	Teacher shares examples of when she notices I provide examples of central idea in my assignments and tests.
Attainable	I feel this is doable.	I am demonstrating my abilities to analyze the central idea.	My teacher is noticing my abilities to share the central idea during class questions, and in our written assignments.
Results oriented	Reflect to see that I had the check marks for each part of the central idea.	I remembered the character and the setting, and supporting details, but forgot the plot one time.	Did my teacher notice my efforts in identifying the central idea?
Time bound	I will do this during this unit, prior to and just after the assessment of this standard.	I did this on both writing assignments the teacher assigned.	Did I receive feedback at least twice during this unit on central idea?

Figure 3.4: Sample SMART goals sheet.

My Goal	Strategy or Strategies I Will Try	My Time Line	My Progress	My Notes
Increase my understanding and use of prepositions.	Keep a daily count of prepositions I see or hear for two days.	Two days	I noticed halfway through the day that I hadn't monitored prepositions, so I started at 1 p.m. on Tuesday.	I will keep track on my phone in the notes section. I may have to wait until the end of class so I don't get distracted or in trouble.
			I placed a sticky note on my mirror in the bathroom to remind me on Wednesday to count prepositions.	That worked. I heard twenty-eight prepositions from my teachers. I read thirty-two more in my reading assignments.
		Three days	I did it one more day, since I forgot most of the first day.	I can't believe how I see and hear so many prepositions. I think I am more aware, and I can use variations better now.

Figure 3.5: Sample student action plan.

Reviewing and Reflecting on the Goal Regularly

The third part of the goal-setting process is to review one's progress toward the goal (or goals) and reflect on the action plan. Encourage students to keep their action plans in a prominent place in their binders or in the notes section of their tablets or smartphones, a place that will remind them of their goals frequently. Encourage students to reference their goals and think about them often. On a regular basis, ask students (or have them ask themselves), "Are you still going down the right path?" or "Have any variables changed that will affect your plan?" (Barile, 2015).

Provide students with regular time and resources for self-assessing and self-regulating. This is a great time to track student progress, as students can use their action plans to visually see their goal and their progress toward it. Have students consider questions such as, Where am I in relation to the different points on the proficiency scale? Was my goal *really* achievable, or should I amend it? What evidence can I use to demonstrate attainment of my goal (or lack thereof)? This process allows students to move toward the type of learning Kallick and Zmuda (2017) suggested when they encouraged teachers "to move from 'learning' that is a series of episodic events to learning that is rich with connection and continuity" (p. 38). You may also have students review websites or apps, check with other students for their strategies, and provide other ideas for helping themselves self-monitor. The timeframe for holding these self-assessment sessions will vary, based on the nature of the time in the classroom and the age of students, but a good rule of thumb is to hold sessions weekly to biweekly.

Students may benefit from having a group goal-setting chart visible in the classroom. Figure 3.6 provides an example of such a chart, which demonstrates how goal setting is an ongoing process. Each student writes a goal on a sticky note, which he or she then displays on a chart and revises weekly. Because these goals are on sticky notes, students can easily move and modify them as students reflect on them and track progress.

We all become stronger by setting goals!					
	Student A	Student B	Student C	Student D	Student E
Week 1	I will practice my vocabulary words at home.	I will get faster at the pace in physical education.	I will finish my persuasion writing by Thursday.	I will practice my facts at home this week.	I will practice my spelling words every night.
Week 2					
Week 3					

Figure 3.6: Example of a goal-setting chart.

Visit MarzanoResources.com/reproducibles for a free reproducible version of this figure.

Encourage students to work toward progress, not perfection. Typically, improvement takes time. Early into the process, students may not be able to accomplish all the items on their action plans. When the focus is on progress, rather than perfection, students are more likely to maintain a positive perspective, celebrate achievements, and continue persevering toward their goals.

Another way to keep goal setting and progress monitoring meaningful is for teachers to reflect on their own practices as they engage students in the goal-setting process (Farrell et al., 2015). Consider your purpose when engaging students with feedback.

- How are you providing time for students to reflect on feedback?
- What processes have you taught students to help them when reacting to feedback or providing it to others?
- Are your practices more in line with mastery or comparison orientation?
- How might you change an activity for another group or class?

As teachers, the goal is to move from comparison to more mastery-oriented goals and growth mindsets. By reflecting on the aforementioned questions, teachers will be cognizant of their classroom practices and how they are fostering the type of goal setting for their students.

Consider also how you wish to share student goals with parents. Students can place goals into electronic formats for parents or use existing structures for school-home communication. The key is to not only share with parents the performance (grade or summative score) but also the progress (or lack thereof) toward goals the student sets. Focusing on an action plan encourages students and parents to collaborate when considering strategies for attaining a goal. It fosters student ownership and hope and often lessens resentment and fear.

It would be futile for students to set goals without then focusing on their progress toward those goals over time. Consequently, the remainder of this chapter will focus on strategies for tracking individual and classwide progress toward student goals.

Tracking Progress

Students tracking their progress is another important part of a standards-based learning environment. In fact, in fourteen controlled studies conducted at Marzano Research (since renamed Marzano Resources), this practice is associated with a 32 percentile-point gain in student achievement (Marzano, 2010). Tracking progress may be as simple as a student using a piece of graph paper to track scores over time, or it might be more in depth, involving students tracking their progress against specific learning targets. In either case, learning to track progress is a transferrable, metacognitive skill. Douglas Fisher and Nancy Frey (2007) reiterated, "When teachers become more deliberate in the ways they check for understanding, they model the metacognitive awareness learners need to develop" (p. 135). Such an awareness empowers students to know, monitor, and act on their own progress. The message sent is that the *process* of learning is more important than the finality of a grade. Many students have reduced school into a series of correct or incorrect ways to answer test questions. They equate success as an ability to memorize and discharge information via a plethora of tests, which may or may not truly represent knowledge and understanding. Learning is more personal and meaningful when students have the time and expectations to track their progress.

Students tracking their own progress should coincide with teachers tracking student progress. In fact, the data teachers obtain from assessments to inform planning and instruction should be, in many ways, similar to the information they share with students. This might include how many and what types of questions the student responded to correctly or incorrectly. For instance, if test items one through four are at level 2.0 for a specific standard, a student who gets those correct easily sees her ability to perform the necessary prerequisite skills for that standard. When a student also gets virtually all of items six through twelve correct—items at a level 3.0 for a particular standard—she knows she is performing proficiently on that same standard. By using this method, students see assessment as work that exemplifies their knowledge and skills for a standard, rather than an accumulation of item points, a raw score, or a generic grade. This process is detailed later in the assessment chapter (page 71). The teacher or student might also review the incorrect items and complete an assignment correction process to include:

1. What is the correct answer?

2. Why is that answer correct?

3. Why was my answer incorrect?

Of course there are instances when teachers will have information that students should not. For instance, students should not know exactly how every other student performed on the very same assessment or assignment, as that information would be confidential.

The following sections will provide teachers and students with tools to track both individual and classwide progress toward student-generated goals.

Tracking Individual Progress

There are many ways to encourage students to track their individual progress. As stated previously, progress tracking can be as simple as using a piece of graph paper and having students track the scores they receive during a unit, quarter, trimester, or semester. It could also be a separate form like the one in figure 3.7 (page 64), where a student not only tracks proficiency scale scores along the left-hand column but also connects those scores to different assessments and the dates noted on the right side. When using this form, the student is aware of his or her progress toward a goal, as noted where the student lists his or her score at the beginning (typically from some sort of preassessment) and then also where the student adds a goal for 3.0 by November 17.

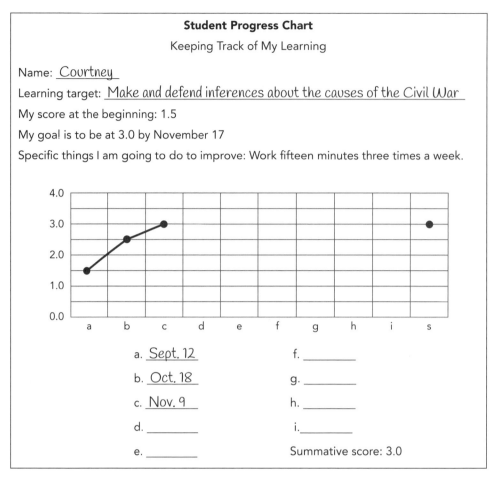

Source: Adapted from Marzano, 2010.

Figure 3.7: Student progress chart.

Encouraging students to track progress might even be a bit more detailed, as the form in figure 3.8 shows. In this format, there is a space for the student to list the learning target, beginning score, and goal score, and also space for the student to personalize the proficiency scale levels into his or her own words toward the bottom. This example is a more sophisticated way for students to track progress using various assessments, scale scores, and corresponding proficiency descriptors. Additionally, it provides ideas for teachers regarding any necessary extra support or extensions for students throughout the tracking process.

On occasion, teachers track classwide progress in addition to individual student growth. The following section focuses on strategies and considerations for tracking class progress.

Tracking Student Progress

Desired student responses: Explaining the class's progress on specific learning targets

Extra support: Describing specific elements of a proficiency scale on which the whole class is doing well and specific elements on which the whole class needs more work

Extension: Asking students who perform specific elements of a proficiency scale well to give feedback and advice to students who need help with the same measurement topic

---

Tracking My Own Learning

Student name: _____ Class: _____ Date: _____

Learning target: _____

_____

My beginning score: _____ My goal score: _____ by: _____

4.0							
3.0							
2.0							
1.0							
0.0							
	A	B	C	D	E	F	G

Assessment dates:

A _____

B _____

C _____

D _____

E _____

F _____

G _____

Proficiency Scale

4.0
3.0
2.0
1.0

Source: Adapted from Marzano, 2016.

Figure 3.8: Form for tracking student progress.

*Visit **MarzanoResources.com/reproducibles** for a free reproducible version of this figure.*

Tracking Class Progress

Some teachers may find it beneficial for whole classes to track their progress. In this scenario, students will see how their own performance fares compared with the other students in class (and potentially other classes as well). Assigning a student a specific sticker may be one way to do this, so student names are not indicated on the chart. As noted earlier in this chapter, this is comparison-oriented feedback. Although it is not necessarily a poor option, it does require a sense of classroom and school culture in which teachers and students clearly understand that learning is a process, and that some students will learn certain things faster and to a greater degree than others. This in no way makes one student better or worse than another; the students are simply different in their learning pace and understanding. Also, this method requires teachers to cultivate a culture about learning that notes virtually all students will likely experience times when they are accelerating through a learning target, and other times when they may need more support. In this manner, comparison may be positively motivating and something to consider tracking.

Refer to figure 3.9 for one method for tracking class progress. This chart displays the average assignment scores of students in a class on the *x*-axis. The *y*-axis depicts the percentage of students at or above proficiency. This helps students to be mindful of their progress in comparison to that of others in their class.

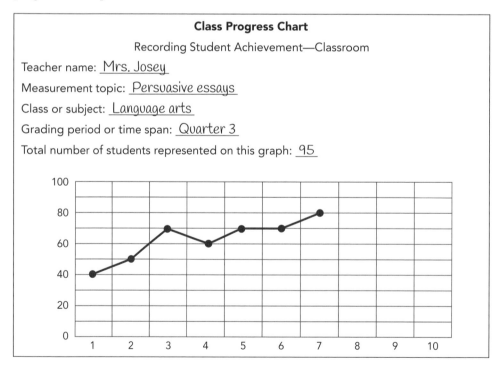

Class Progress Chart

Recording Student Achievement—Classroom

Teacher name: Mrs. Josey

Measurement topic: Persuasive essays

Class or subject: Language arts

Grading period or time span: Quarter 3

Total number of students represented on this graph: 95

1. 1/12 holiday celebrations essay	6. 3/8 seasonal essay
2. 1/23 pollution essay	7. 3/21 environmental essay
3. 2/3 presidential essay	8. _____
4. 2/14 valentine essay	9. _____
5. 2/29 scientific theory essay	10. _____

Source: Adapted from Marzano, 2006.

Figure 3.9: Class progress chart.

Figure 3.10 (page 68) lists the various assignments, learning targets, or both, for students to master across the top of the chart. The descriptors in the left column depict the level of proficiency. Anonymous student indicators, shown here as the letter *X*, could also be numbers or stickers. They indicate where students are in relation to the rest of the class for the various learning targets.

Again, it's important to note that using more overt comparisons requires a learning culture where students (and teachers) understand that they are not permanently labeled because of a level of proficiency on a learning target. Rather, students should understand that learning may take more or less time for some.

As we note in the many examples, tracking progress goes hand-in-hand with goal setting. As students become aware of their progress toward important learning targets, they can more effectively set meaningful goals.

Celebrating Success Toward Goals

As students work toward and obtain the goals they set, teachers should be sure to celebrate these accomplishments. Teachers may want to recognize students' goal attainment in various ways. One might be to simply have students share their portfolios of work and goals with another student. Teachers could provide students with sample questions to ask one another and even sample phrases of compliment or suggestion to enable appropriate dialogue in this situation. This is the perfect place to insert the reflective questions or prompts addressed previously in the chapter. For example:

- "I'm getting much better at . . ."
- "I'm still not sure how to . . ."
- "The part I find the most difficult was . . ."
- "How would you do things differently next time?"
- "What helped you when _____ got tricky?"

Another strategy may include sharing student progress and goals regularly with parents, providing places for comments and next considerations. This school-home connection helps inform parents about not only what is being taught but also how their child

Learning Target / Proficiency Level	Draw a molecular structure.	Determine bond polarity.	Identify type of intermolecular forces (IMF) in a compound.	Determine polarity of a molecule.	Determine shape of a molecule.	Determine how IMF affects boiling and melting points.	Understand freezing point and boiling point depression.
Advanced	XXX	XX	XXXXXXX	XXXXXX	XXXXX		
Proficient	XXXXXXXXXX	XXXXXXXXX	XXXXXXXXX	XXXXXXXXXX	XXXXXXXXX		
Progressing	XX	XXX	XX				

Source: Adapted from © 2006 by Erik Prouty.

Figure 3.10: Sample class progress chart.

is performing. Formalizing this process to use during parent-teacher conferences may be a more thorough and thoughtful connection.

Additionally, students may use their goal-progress charts to write a descriptive or argumentative essay as to why they have achieved results toward the learning targets of the course or discipline. Students may also create a compare-and-contrast diagram noting where they are in their own learning compared to others in the class or classes. These are reflective documents that may help students see their growth. Students may elect to share them with others or post them on a bulletin board. Whichever method they choose, teacher and students should note and celebrate their success in achieving their goal to encourage repeat behavior.

Summary

No matter the form or format, communicating learning in more accurate and student-focused ways is important in a standards-based learning environment. Goal setting and tracking student progress are imperative for student ownership in the learning process. It is essential to model the goal-setting process, teach students specific processes for setting goals and strategies for attaining them, and infuse the review and revision of goals into regular classroom practice. When students are clear about the importance of learning targets through the use of proficiency scales, they can more accurately and meaningfully track their progress individually and even as a class. Using this information to teach students how to set personal learning targets is the transportable skill students will use throughout life. In the following chapter, we focus our attention on administering quality classroom assessments and the complexity of figuring grades.

Administering Quality Classroom Assessments and Figuring Grades

Once the teacher prioritizes standards and develops proficiency scales, and students have set goals and tracked their progress, the teacher is poised for the next critical step in a standards-based learning environment—assessing learners. Assessment is an essential part of the learning process; it must occur for teachers to know how well students are acquiring the knowledge and skills articulated on the proficiency scales. As one high school principal stated:

> Utilizing standards-based grading practices allows teachers to truly differentiate instruction, because activities and assessments can be planned around students' levels of knowledge as they are defined by the scale. As teachers assess progress, students are able to learn and grow at a pace that is appropriate to their learning. (W. Barnes, personal communication, January 19, 2018)

As with classroom instruction, there are multiple ways a teacher can choose to assess student achievement. This is possible when a teacher considers assessment as anything a teacher does to gather information about what a student knows and is able to do. While assessing learners is hardly new to the educational environment, effective assessment practice is more than *testing* students every once in a while, most commonly at the end of an instructional unit. We suggest that assessments occur on a more frequent basis in order to carefully monitor growth, rather than simply being done at the end of a lesson or unit.

In this chapter, we will present several types of assessment teachers may use in a standards-based classroom before discussing special considerations in scoring assessments and figuring summative grades using proficiency scales. It will also provide guidance on dealing with unusual patterns of student performance and handling extra credit and assessment retakes.

Understanding the Types of Assessment

The act of testing students has been part of classroom practice for many years. As time has passed and educators have learned more about effective classroom practice, they have gained collective understanding that a teacher can do more than simply give a test to learn about what students know and are able to do. In *Formative Assessment & Standards-Based Grading*, Marzano (2010) presents three types of assessments. He suggests that standards-based classrooms should include a combination of the three types of assessment so that learners experience a balanced assessment approach. These three types of assessment include (1) obtrusive, (2) unobtrusive, and (3) student-generated assessments. We agree that standards-based learning should provide students with multiple and varied ways to show their knowledge and skill.

Obtrusive Assessment

Obtrusive assessment is formal in nature and is the type that is most test-like. Unit or chapter tests, quizzes, projects, and in-class assignments are all examples of obtrusive assessment. A defining characteristic of obtrusive assessment is that it interrupts the instructional process, thereby making certain students are fully aware that an important classroom event is occurring. Following the administration and scoring of obtrusive assessment, the teacher usually records student scores in his or her gradebook. In traditional classrooms, scores on obtrusive assessments are percentage scores, based on the one-hundred-point scale. In a standards-based environment, proficiency scales are the basis of the assessment. This allows the teacher to align the performance score with the scores on the proficiency scale.

There are multiple possibilities for how obtrusive assessments may be structured in a standards-based classroom. Regardless of the assessment structure a teacher chooses, he or she must give students the opportunity to engage in items at all three levels on the proficiency scale (2.0–4.0) at some point during the unit. Especially on obtrusive assessments, teachers commonly use traditional item types (such as true/false, matching, multiple choice, fill-in-the-blank, short answer, and extended response). Regardless of the type of assessment a teacher chooses for monitoring progress on proficiency scales, it is critical that items and tasks are high quality. Table 4.1 depicts the most commonly used item types when assessing learners in a formal manner, as well as attributes of high-quality items.

It is very common for a teacher to use a combination of selected-response and constructed-response items to design obtrusive assessments. Selected-response items are usually best suited for score 2.0 content on the proficiency scale, while constructed-response items (including extended response) typically work best with score 3.0 and score 4.0 content.

Sometimes, a teacher may choose to write an obtrusive assessment that includes traditional item types for all score levels on the proficiency scale that include academic content, especially when a teacher wants to administer a formal end-of-unit assessment.

Table 4.1: Common Item Types and Their Attributes

Item Type	Description of High-Quality Items
Selected-Response Items	
True/False	• Keep statements related to a single concept. • Be certain statements are completely true or completely false. • Avoid using double negatives. • Refrain from qualifiers like *some* or *most*. • Use cautiously, as students have a 50 percent chance of guessing correctly.
Matching	• Keep the content within the same context (all dates, all ideas, all names). • Maintain short sets of roughly seven or fewer items per grouping. • Use an uneven number of options. • Consider using items multiple times to lessen options for process of elimination. • Ensure the longer reading portion is on the left, with the shorter response options on the right.
Multiple Choice	• State the stem in the positive, when possible. • Emphasize any qualifying language like *always*, *sometimes*, and *never*. • Be certain all options are conceivable. • Keep length consistent. • Avoid allowing grammar to give away a response (for example, *an* or *a*). • Ensure there is one best answer.
Constructed-Response Items	
Fill-in-the-Blank	• Place the blank toward the end of the statement to provide context to the student. • Limit the number of blanks (1–2) within a single item. • Keep blanks the same length so as to not give away longer or shorter responses. • Be mindful of using word banks, as it may lessen the difficulty of the item.
Short Answer and Extended Repose	• Be certain what you request is clear to the reader (for example, numbers or an explanation). • Develop and communicate scoring criteria ahead of time. • Provide adequate and similar space for responses. • Review prompts for elements of bias.

Source: Adapted from Gareis & Grant, 2008.

For example, consider a proficiency scale for comparing fractions that includes the score 2.0 target, "The student will recall the meaning of the word *denominator*." An item on an obtrusive assessment for this target might be the following:

> Does the word *denominator* refer to the top or bottom number on a fraction?

This item provides insight as to whether or not a student has adequate understanding of an important vocabulary term. The teacher can address other vocabulary terms in additional score 2.0 items, as well as other simple content targets. The same practice occurs at scores 3.0 and 4.0. Figure 4.1 shows the score 2.0 example as well as sample 3.0 and 4.0 targets on a proficiency scale for comparing fractions, and also possible assessment items relating to these learning targets.

Proficiency Scale Levels	Aligned Assessment Items
Score 2.0: The student will recall the meaning of the word *denominator*.	Does the word *denominator* refer to the top or bottom number on a fraction?
Score 3.0: The student will justify the comparison of two fractions with different denominators.	Determine whether the correct symbol has been chosen to compare the two fractions. Then, explain why you made your choice.
Score 4.0: The student will order three fractions with different numerators and denominators and explain the process he or she used.	Order the following three fractions from least to greatest. Then, explain how you made your decision. $\frac{6}{8}$ $\frac{4}{9}$ $\frac{5}{10}$

Figure 4.1: Sample learning targets and assessment items.

Many teachers like this approach to obtrusive assessment because it communicates to students that there will be no unexpected items on the assessment and that each item connects to a target on the proficiency scale. This implies that the teacher has familiarized students with the proficiency scale during the opportunity to learn and that students understand that the proficiency scale is the basis of all learning activities associated with it, including assessments. Another reason teachers often like this approach is because when simple content items are presented first on the obtrusive assessment, students often begin the assessment with a higher degree of confidence. Finally, this approach to formal assessment gives a valuable data point for making decisions about the type of instructional supports students need at that point in time.

Sometimes a teacher may view it worthwhile to preassess learners on the proficiency scale content. (See Administering the Preassessment, page 36.) This preassessment process provides information about students' current knowledge *before* it provides the opportunity to learn and allows the teacher to form flexible groups on existing knowledge and skill.

Once the teacher forms flexible groups, he or she plans specific instruction based on the information learned through the preassessment process.

Assessments developed for preassessment typically include a minimal number of items and don't always (but may) include an item for score 4.0 on the proficiency scale. The following vignette provides an example of a preassessment for grade 4 students on the measurement topic of *story elements.*

Mr. Jonas is preparing to provide the opportunity to learn about story elements to his fourth-grade students. He knows the importance of students mastering this priority standard, so he decides to preassess his learners to establish some flexible groups based on their current understanding of *character*, *setting*, or *event* in a story or drama. His hope with implementing the strategy of flexible groups is that students will receive the best support he can provide to ensure they all show growth over time. His pretest consists of only four items, with at least one item related to each of the three levels on the proficiency scale. By using only four items, he is confident that he will glean information about students' current level of knowledge without using excessive instructional time.

Mr. Jonas explains to his students the preassessment's purpose and that he really needs their very best effort on the reading of the passage and their responses to the four items. He also tells the students that he knows they may not know the answers to every item yet, and he reassures them that this is just fine. As the pretest is occurring, Mr. Jonas responds to questions from individual students and reminds the class that he needs its best effort. After the administration of the pretest, Mr. Jonas scores the preassessment and uses the information to group students based on their current understanding of story elements.

The flexible groups that Mr. Jonas forms are not permanent, but only established for the purpose of differentiating instruction to meet the instructional needs of students within each small group.

Sometimes a teacher may decide to assess a single level on a proficiency scale rather than provide items that cover the entirety of the scale as described in the preceding vignette. This practice might be either a pretest opportunity or just occur for the sake of determining whether or not students have already acquired understanding of the simple content. For example, a scale for the measurement topic of figurative language might include the score 2.0 target, "The student will identify examples of alliteration, hyperbole, metaphor, onomatopoeia, personification, and simile in isolation." In order to assess this simple content, the following item might be on a short obtrusive assessment.

Which type of figurative language is represented in the statement, "Boom! The thunder echoed through the sky"?

a. alliteration

b. hyperbole

c. personification

d. onomatopeia

The teacher would include additional, similar items as well, so that he or she can gain understanding of whether students learn the foundational knowledge. Score 2.0 is the highest score possible on this assessment.

Finally, there are times when teachers want to assess multiple priority standards on a single obtrusive assessment, typically at the end of an instructional unit. When a teacher chooses this practice, he or she must remember to limit the number of standards he or she assesses to keep the length of the assessment manageable. This usually means including no more than three or four standards on a single obtrusive assessment. Additionally, if the teacher assesses multiple standards, he or she should assign multiple scores—one for each standard on the assessment. This ensures that students know where to apply future effort in order to increase their understanding of the content.

While teachers typically like the obtrusive assessment practices previously described, there is valid reasoning to present such traditional item types to students on an assessment in random order, as opposed to ordering them by proficiency scale levels. In fact, some teachers prefer to refrain from offering any information to students about the levels on the proficiency scale in relation to individual items. This is certainly acceptable practice, but it is still very important that all items on the assessment align with language on the proficiency scale. In classrooms that use proficiency scales frequently, students can oftentimes determine which level on the scale each item is measuring—which is positive!

Effective classroom assessments include more than traditional item types. Teachers may also use one or several of the following for informing decisions about levels of student mastery.

- **Probing discussions:** This involves the teacher engaging in a conversation about the content on a proficiency scale with an individual student or small group of students.

- **Observations:** This requires the teacher to deliberately watch a student for specific actions required by language on a proficiency scale. It may also be that a teacher is watching a student's body language to learn about his or her comfort with a task assigned.

- **Demonstrations:** This type of assessment requires a student to show his or her knowledge or skill by producing something or performing in some way.

Additionally, teachers should consider giving students the opportunity to suggest how they want teachers to assess them. When teachers use a variety of assessment types in the classroom and items and tasks are high quality, we propose that teachers' judgments regarding student achievement will be very accurate. As teachers gather accurate data about current levels of achievement, they can make appropriate decisions and provide instructional support for each learner in the environment.

While formal assessments are common in classrooms, informal assessments are also crucial in determining a student's placement on a proficiency scale. The next section will discuss unobtrusive assessment.

Unobtrusive Assessment

A second type of assessment that a teacher can use to monitor student progress is *unobtrusive assessment* (Marzano, 2010). As the prefix *un* implies, this type of assessment is not formal and, therefore, is not test-like. It is even possible that a student may be totally unaware that the teacher is assessing him or her when a teacher chooses to use unobtrusive assessment. While a teacher deliberately plans for obtrusive assessment, he or she often spontaneously implements unobtrusive assessment or uses it on the fly. This makes it very possible to use unobtrusive assessment on an on-demand basis to determine individual student knowledge or skill.

There are numerous ways a teacher can administer unobtrusive assessments, with the most common being observations and personal communication with students. A teacher can learn much about what a student knows by watching him or her and then recording the results of that observation. Teachers can enhance this type of unobtrusive assessment when they combine personal communication with the observation. Imagine the following scenario.

Mrs. Jameson has five stations set up in her classroom for collecting information about what her students know about a particular learning target within their social studies unit on the Civil War. She organizes her students into groups of four and then assigns each a starting station. She posted a question on a chart paper at each location. Mrs. Jameson also provides a recording sheet for each student and gives the direction that they are to determine an accurate response for the question and then record that response on the sheet. After she completes giving directions, Mrs. Jameson spends time with each of the five groups, listening to their conversations and observing individual students as to whether or not they are able to contribute to the conversation. Periodically, she will ask a specific student a probing question in order to learn more about what he or she knows. At the end of the activity, she considers all the information she collected about individual students and records a score related to the proficiency scale for each student in the gradebook. She will use this score to determine a summative score for the appropriate measurement topic.

Additional unobtrusive assessment examples may include:

- **Teacher-student conferences**—Teacher-student discussions with probing questions related to content on a proficiency scale

- **Journal entries**—Student writing related to a teacher-provided prompt that offers insight into understanding of content on a proficiency scale

- **Inside-outside circle**—A question-and-answer discussion structure that allows the teacher to listen in for key ideas for students to articulate

- **Line-ups**—Another question-and-answer discussion structure that involves students forming two lines facing one another (similar to inside-outside circle)

- **Student notebooks**—An ongoing collection of student work compiled in a single location (sometimes called a portfolio of work)

- **Tallies of student contributions to class discussions**—A record of student input to class discussion for the purpose of considering student understanding of content

- **Think-pair-share**—A discussion structure that allows the teacher to listen in for key ideas for students to share

It is important to remember that following each of these unobtrusive assessment opportunities, the teacher should record a score related to the correlating proficiency scale. For example, a teacher might facilitate an inside-outside circle that requires students to respond to teacher-provided questions relating to level 2.0 on a proficiency scale. As the discussion occurs, the teacher can listen to responses provided by a student and determine whether or not he or she has acquired the knowledge required by this level on the scale. If the knowledge has been acquired, the teacher can record a score of 2.0 in the gradebook for this particular student. It is important to note that not all students would receive the exact same scores since not all students would be assessed in this manner by the teacher.

One of the most positive attributes of unobtrusive assessment is its degree of accuracy. Because students are often unaware that the teacher is conducting assessment, the anxiety and nervousness that often accompanies obtrusive (formal) assessment is not present. This leads to more accurate results regarding what students know and are able to do. Despite this positive attribute, many teachers neglect using unobtrusive assessment to determine grades. In fact, teachers don't oftentimes record the results of unobtrusive assessment in the gradebook. However, as individual teachers learn more about different assessment types, they typically realize how valuable informal assessment is and begin to deliberately plan for integrating more and more of it into their daily instruction.

A final type of assessment is the less-structured student-generated assessment. The following section discusses this assessment type and its uses.

Student-Generated Assessment

The third type of assessment is *student-generated assessment* (Marzano, 2010). As the name implies, when a teacher utilizes this type, the student generates an idea for how he or she wants to demonstrate understanding of the content. Although this assessment type is underused, teachers who include it in their classroom assessment practice profess that it fosters a high level of engagement, mostly due to the ownership the student feels as a result of determining the assessment method.

There are multiple ways that teachers can implement student-generated assessment in the classroom. The following vignette describes two common approaches to its use: (1) To inform about a student's current level of performance and (2) to provide students the opportunity to attain level 4.0 on a proficiency scale.

Miss Grimley is a sixth-grade mathematics teacher who uses student-generated assessment in multiple ways in her classroom. Sometimes, she is unsure of a particular student's current level of performance on a proficiency scale. When this is the case, she offers the student a student-generated assessment opportunity. This particular situation presented itself recently with Zack, who had performed inconsistently on previous assessments for multiplying and dividing fractions. In order to be more confident about whether or not he had attained the knowledge and skill at score 3.0, Miss Grimley engaged in a conversation with Zack about how he might show her that he was most definitely proficient on this scale. Zack accepted the invitation for Miss Grimley to assess him again. His idea was to come to the classroom after school that day to work a few problems on the whiteboard in order to demonstrate mastery of this important content. Zack showed up at 3:30 p.m., at which time Miss Grimley had prepared four problems for Zack to complete. At the conclusion of his work, she was able to congratulate him on his success and to move forward with confidence that he was able to multiply and divide fractions!

Miss Grimley also offers student-generated assessment opportunities to students who have already mastered the score 3.0 content on a scale. She schedules an individual meeting with each student who is ready to attempt score 4.0. During this meeting, she and the student discuss possible assessment activities. Once the student makes a decision about the assessment, he or she receives time to complete the task. This student-generated task allows for Miss Grimley to make an accurate decision about whether or not the student is able to work at the knowledge application level. This teacher has discovered that students are more likely to attempt score 4.0 when they have the opportunity to make decisions about the assessment itself.

Some teachers use menu-choice boards to help with decision making about the student-generated assessment task. Figure 4.2 is an example of a menu board. Prior to sharing the menu board with students, a teacher would determine appropriate assessment tasks related to a proficiency scale. Once the teacher has generated all items on the menu board, the teacher provides a brief description of each option and then allows students to choose which option they want to complete.

Write a set of steps for comparing two fractions with different denominators.	Choose two of the five problems provided for comparing fractions.	Create a mathematics rap or rhyme that explains how to compare two fractions with different denominators.
Create and solve a word problem that requires the learner to compare two fractions with different denominators.	Do student-choice activity (with teacher approval).	Create a word puzzle using the vocabulary related to comparing fractions.
Complete page 37 in your mathematics workbook.	Develop a game that requires the players to compare fractions with like and unlike denominators.	Identify three examples of how to use the skill of comparing fractions in the real world.

Figure 4.2: Sample menu board.

Another possible use of student-generated assessment occurs when a teacher needs an additional data point to make a confident inference about student achievement. Consider a student who has the following scores related to a measurement topic: 2.0, 2.0, 2.5, 3.0. A teacher might approach a student in this scenario and offer a student-generated assessment opportunity in order to more confidently discern the student's current level of performance. The teacher invites the student to suggest how he or she might prove that score 3.0 is more accurate than 2.5. Sometimes the process of negotiation occurs between teacher and student to determine the assessment method. If the student earns a score 3.0 on the student-generated assessment, the teacher has the proof he or she needs to assign a summative score of 3.0. A score of 2.5 may be more accurate if the student earns a score 2.5 or lower.

The preceding example shows scoring assessments in a standards-based classroom has unique challenges not present in a traditional classroom. The following section discusses special considerations for scoring assessments.

Scoring Assessments

Teachers must consider several aspects when scoring assessments based on proficiency scales. Three issues for teachers to be aware of are (1) response patterns, (2) item weighting, and (3) response codes.

Response Patterns

Figure 4.3, based on Marzano (2010), displays a sample student response pattern for items on an assessment. It shows the number of items for each level on the proficiency scale and the individual student's performance.

Proficiency Scale Level	Total Number of Items	Items Answered Correctly
Score 2.0	6	5
Score 3.0	4	2
Score 4.0	1	0

Source: Marzano, 2010.

Figure 4.3: Sample assessment response pattern.

To score the assessment, the teacher simply examines the pattern of student responses. Since the student answers the majority of the level 2.0 items correctly, it is clear that he or she has acquired understanding of the score 2.0 content on the scale. The student only responds to half of the level 3.0 items correctly and does not answer the level 4.0 item right. Therefore, the most accurate score for this assessment is a 2.5.

Item Weighting

Another issue to be aware of is item weighting. When examining individual items on an assessment, there are two methods that a teacher might use to denote how a student responds to each item. The first assigns points, or weights, to individual items. Simple items such as multiple-choice questions might only be worth one point. As the teacher scores a student's response, a correct answer would earn the student one point while an incorrect answer would earn zero points. In contrast, the second method is an extended-response item that requires students to access multiple pieces of information might be worth four points. As the teacher reads a student's response, he or she must decide how many of the available four points the student earned. The teacher records the points the student earned on each item and compares them to the points available in order to assign an overall score. See figure 4.4 (page 82, based on a concept by Marzano et al., 2016), for an example of item weighting.

When reviewing the points the student earned compared to the points available, the teacher can easily see that the student has earned all the available points at score 2.0, about half the available points for score 3.0, and none of the points available for score 4.0. Therefore, score 2.5 is probably the most accurate representation of the student's knowledge at this point. It is important to note that a scoring guide is useful for scoring items that are assigned points. A scoring guide will include a brief description of what type of answer receives a score of 5 when the teacher assigns five points to an item, and so on.

Proficiency Scale Level	Item Number	Points Available	Points Earned
Score 2.0	1	1	1
	2	1	1
	3	1	1
	4	1	1
	5	1	1
	6	1	1
Total		6	6
Score 3.0	7	2	2
	8	2	1
	9	2	1
	10	3	1
Total		9	5
Score 4.0	11	5	0
Total		5	0

Source: Marzano et al., 2016.

Figure 4.4: Scoring assessments with points.

Response Codes

The final issue is response codes. With response codes, the teacher describes each student response as *correct* (C), *partially correct* (PC), or *incorrect* (I). After scoring the assessment items, the teacher determines the overall score for the assessment based on the pattern of student responses. Figure 4.5 (based on concepts from Marzano, 2010) shows an example of using response codes.

This student performance—correct at score 2.0, partially correct at score 3.0, and incorrect at score 4.0—suggests that the student has earned a score 2.5.

Figuring Grades

Perhaps the most challenging aspect of moving to a standards-based learning environment from a more traditional classroom comes in the form of determining student grades. Some aspects of grading will remain the same: for example, teachers will assess students and monitor their progress. Teachers will likely use many of the assessment items that they may have been using for years with standards-based or standards-referenced grading. But some important aspects will change.

One key difference is the purpose of figuring and reporting grades. In a standards-based learning environment, the concern is less with identifying what a student is doing

Proficiency Scale Level	Item Number	Response Code
Score 2.0	1	C
	2	C
	3	C
	4	C
	5	C
	6	C
Overall Pattern		C
Score 3.0	7	C
	8	PC
	9	PC
	10	I
Overall Pattern		PC
Score 4.0	11	I
Overall Pattern		I

Source: Marzano, 2010.

Figure 4.5: Scoring assessments with response codes.

incorrectly and reporting grades that start at the maximum score and gradually descend as teachers remove portions of the score for incorrect responses. Rather, standards-based grading focuses on the students' current level of success on each of the priority standards, and on helping students identify their next steps in the learning progression for each standard. This represents a fundamental shift in why teachers report student performance, and once students understand that difference, their attitude toward assessment and grading will also change in numerous ways. For example, students will not fear assessment; rather, many students will look forward to the opportunity of determining their growth on the standards they have been using in class. As a result, their entire approach to preparing for assessment will likely change, and teachers may see homework completion rates go up and students studying when teachers did not assign that work!

The remainder of this chapter will identify some important shifts in approaching the assignment of student-performance scores in a standards-based environment. First, we will define two important and connected terms: (1) *scores* and (2) *grades*. There are some distinct differences in what and how scores are used in determining a student's summative grade. Next, we will discuss the use of item response theory (IRT) in designing assessments that better inform the grades students receive. This ensures an assessment isn't classified as too easy or too hard but rather more accurately aligns with the proficiency scale. Then, we address formative and summative assessment, unusual patterns in student performance, and issues surrounding figuring grades with extra credit and retakes.

Scores and Grades

Teachers have assigned grades to student performance as long as there have been teachers and students. However, were we to ask a hundred teachers to describe what a grade is, and what the purpose of grading is, we would receive nearly as many answers as there were respondents. Too often, teachers grade without considering the purpose of grading or what a grade actually represents.

From a standards-based learning perspective, a grade represents a snapshot of student performance on a particular standard, at a particular moment. Given this perspective, it is useful to consider that the scores that assignments and assessments provide—those numbers teachers record in gradebooks—are better termed *scores* than *grades*, since the score better represents the temporary nature of student performance. A score can easily change, hopefully in an upward direction, with the next assessment. Students who focus on the learning progression that the proficiency scales teachers use in class depict, and who set personal goals for their own performance on these proficiency scales, will see their performance much more as scores relative to the proficiency scale. They will focus much less on the grade they are receiving in class if they are aware of their increasing performance on the scores on the proficiency scale.

Thus, by terming the numbers we record as *scores*, and using that term rather than *grades* with students, students can focus on what is truly important—their increasing competence with the standards. Students who focus in that manner have little concern for their grades; frankly, they are already aware of the grade they will get in the class.

Item Response Theory

The standards-based grading process uses the concept of *item response theory* (Marzano, 2010). IRT is a measurement theory that teachers use to assess a student's abilities based on different levels of rigor at which he or she can consistently demonstrate success. The Statistics How-To website (www.statisticshowto.com) explains the concept of IRT in simple terms:

> Item Response Theory (IRT) is a way to analyze responses to tests or questionnaires with the goal of improving measurement accuracy and reliability. If you want your test to actually measure what it is supposed to measure (i.e. mathematical ability, a student's reading ability or historical knowledge), IRT is one way to develop your tests. . . . Item response theory takes into account the number of questions answered correctly *and* the difficulty of the question. The SAT and GRE both use Item Response Theory for their tests.

Assessments constructed to represent the different levels of a proficiency scale make it possible to use the concept of IRT in classroom grading. Students' abilities at different levels of rigor, scored via assessment opportunities correlating to the different levels in a proficiency scale, reveal a clear pattern of understanding. For example, a student's ability to consistently answer questions that measure the level 2.0 content of a proficiency scale would provide the teacher with a pattern of successful responses that allow the teacher to make an accurate inference and score the student at level 2.0 on the scale. As the student's knowledge grows and he or she demonstrates the ability to consistently be successful with level 3.0 or level 4.0 content items, the teacher can clearly see and know his or her ability via the IRT concept.

We should note that while assessments are tied to their respective proficiency scales, not all assessments include items specifically designed to measure student performance on a particular level of the scale. Many assessments can measure student performance on a more global basis and are particularly useful when students are demonstrating abilities on a particular skill. Examples of assessments of this type include student performance of physical education skills, drama and music performances, creation of artistic pieces, and essays. In these cases, the proficiency scale provides levels of performance that the teacher judges, using the scale as a rubric. In many other cases, though, items on an assessment would typically be tied to specific performance levels on the proficiency scales.

Formative Assessment and Summative Assessment

Some educators think of differences they may have learned between formative assessments and summative assessments for such scores. We purposefully simplify and use the language of a *score*. We don't specify whether or not it is a formative assessment or summative assessment. A score is anything a teacher uses to inform where a student is on his or her learning journey. For instance, a score might be a quiz, an assessment, a project, a writing sample, and maybe an assignment. Educational psychologist John Biggs (1998) reiterated this point, stating, "Sensible educational models make effective use of both FA [formative assessment] and SA [summative assessment]" (p. 105). We certainly suggest teachers use scores that are indicative of the student's actual performance. Scores from assignments and assessments that align with proficiency scales measure student performance on the associated standards, and, thus, are appropriate for teachers to record in the gradebook.

What scores should teachers record in the gradebook? As we will describe in this section, teachers assemble a body of evidence to determine current student performance on a standard, with these multiple data points constituting a larger and more valid body of evidence than a single score alone. We recommend including both formative and summative data points rather than just summative assessment scores to avoid placing a great deal of weight on a few summative data points. Marzano (2018) reiterated this point when he conferred, "The obvious problem with this approach is evident from the discussion about standard error of measurement. The score a student receives on any summative assessment contains error" (p. 73). Error is inherent in any assessment. Even large-scale exams have error. For instance, the error on the ACT is one to two points, depending on the section. ACT (2017) disclosed:

> Rather than representing a precise point, test scores are estimates of a student's educational development. Students should think of their true achievement on the ACT as being within a range that extends

about one standard error of measurement—or about 1 point for the Composite and writing scores, and 2 points for STEM, ELA, and other test scores—above and below their scores. (p. 4)

A special situation sometimes emerges when teachers consider whether to include homework in the gradebook. Homework assignments may not be reflective of a student's independent work. It is possible for other students, parents, or internet sources to strongly influence the work completed during homework assignments. Therefore, we recommend using scores that are most indicative of a student's independent work during class. Marzano (2018) said, "Any time a teacher has information that provides concrete evidence that a particular student is at a particular level on a particular proficiency scale, the teacher should record a score for the student in question" (p. 73). Having said that, some upper-level courses make it difficult to only score students for work completed in class. An example might be an essay written for a high school English course. The likelihood of a student completing all the writing during class is quite slim. Therefore, teachers should employ a variety of strategies to ensure the student actually submits his or her own student work for scoring. One strategy might be for students to complete or share a summary during class of the writing completed as homework, as it is difficult for a student to summarize something the student didn't do.

When it comes to determining a summative grade for a student, teachers should:

- Examine the student's performance on assignments and assessments (mounting evidence)

- Give more weight to recent information (if necessary, discuss the content with the student to shed light on his or her learning progress)

- Limit the use of zeros

- Know the limitations of averaging

- Separate what students know from how they behave

- Acknowledge unique considerations among elementary and secondary schools

These guidelines assist teachers in reaching a more logical and thoughtful summative grade for a student. We will now discuss each of these guidelines in greater detail.

Examining the Student's Performance on Assignments and Assessments

We discussed tracking the student's performance on assignments and assessments in chapter 3 (page 47). The thing to remember is that scores may be based on a variety of evidence that indicates a student's learning. These scores may be from obtrusive assessments, or they may include a collection of informal conversations, unobtrusive assessments, or student-generated examples of evidence. It is important to note that relying heavily on a few assessment scores during a grading period may actually increase the error of the evaluative decision—the summative grade. To arrive at a summative grade the teacher uses the concept of *mounting evidence* by examining the pattern of scores from assessments and assignments for a particular topic or standard. Mounting evidence, as Marzano (2018) described it, is when "the teacher examines the pattern of scores a student has exhibited each time he or she enters a new score in a gradebook. When she feels confident, the teacher then makes an estimate of the student's true score" (p. 74). Teachers should use a series of scores to inform summative grades, rather than depending on a single assessment. Thus, summative grades represent a student's status on a specific topic or standard at some point in time. Figure 4.6 demonstrates the concept of scores and summative grades for a student named Madie, who has taken four assessments for the prioritized standard of *types of business ownership* in her business class.

Prioritized standard: Types of business ownership					
Student Name	Preassessment	Quiz	Mid-Unit Quiz	Test	Summative Grade
Madie	2.0	2.5	3.0	3.0	3.0

Figure 4.6: Sample assessment scores.

The first score is from a preassessment, which only assesses the level 2.0 knowledge and skills in the proficiency scale. She is successful on all items in the assessment, so the teacher assigns her a score of 2.0. The next assessment is a quiz that includes items representing all levels of the proficiency scale. Madie gets all the level 2.0 items correct and some of the level 3.0 items, but not all. The teacher assigns Madie a score of 2.5 because she is demonstrating full knowledge on level 2.0 items but only partial knowledge of the level 3.0 items. The third assessment is a mid-unit quiz, and Madie is successful on all of the level 2.0 and level 3.0 items. The teacher assigns her a score of 3.0. The fourth assessment is a test, and Madie gets all the level 2.0 items and all the level 3.0 items correct, but none of the level 4.0. The teacher assigns a score of 3.0. To assign a summative grade for this topic, the teacher uses the concept of mounting evidence and looks at the pattern of knowledge growth over time. The various scores reveal the pattern of learning and her current level of proficiency: 2.0, 2.5, 3.0, 3.0. Based on these scores, Madie's summative grade for this topic would be 3.0, reflecting her ability to successfully work at the 3.0 level of the scale.

It is important to note the use of the half-step score (2.5) in the previous example. Recall that the half-step scores provide increments of growth for students to recognize their improvement as they gain knowledge but may not have mastered everything at the next level yet. The half-steps promote the concept of growth mindset in the grading process so students understand they are on track and growing in their knowledge and ability. In this manner, standards-based grading does not focus on what a student does wrong but rather on his or her current level of success and where he or she can strive to go next in knowledge gain. This direct correlation of scores to current levels of student knowledge allows students to focus on the learning and not on the point grabbing that is so often a part of a traditional grading approaches.

An important question to consider is how many data points are necessary in order to assign an accurate summative grade. There is no fixed answer to this question. The key question to consider is, "Can I make a confident inference about the learning that has occurred related to this priority standard?" The number of data points necessary for the teacher to be confident in his or her inference will vary from class to class, even from student to student. If a student has demonstrated proficiency on a standard by a set of scores of 3.0 or higher over several assessments, he or she may not need another assessment on this standard, even though other students may require additional assessments.

Giving More Weight to Recent Information

Several researchers discuss giving more weight to recent information (Guskey & Bailey, 2001; O'Connor, 2009). This simply means that as teachers consider what evidence to weigh more heavily, they should give more emphasis to the skills a student displays at later points in time as a good indicator of knowledge and understanding. If necessary, they should discuss the content with the student to better inform their decisions. This seems obvious yet can be such a powerful practice. Consider the following example: Lauren has been working to improve her score in algebra and was recently successful on all of the level 3.0 items in a short formative assessment. The teacher conferences with Lauren and asks her to explain her understanding of the concept now. Lauren successfully explains the concept, and the teacher is reaffirmed in the knowledge that Lauren has reached a proficient level in her understanding of this topic.

As you know, sometimes students demonstrate understanding during classroom discussions or in group activities, yet when they get to an independent obtrusive assessment, they fail to display clarity in understanding. Oftentimes, a brief conversation or probing discussion with a student will better clarify whether or not he or she understands the content to the level of proficiency. If the teacher determines a limited or lack of understanding, he or she would lower the student's scale score. Or, if a teacher discerns a proficient understanding, he or she denotes such when assigning a proficiency score.

Limiting the Use of Zeros

Limiting the use of zeros is an important consideration when teachers are calculating grades using a one hundred–point scale. The concern is that the zero weights so much more heavily in that type of scale than any other grade on the one hundred–point scale, since zeros have a large effect when the teacher uses the mean to measure central tendency. The use of a zero shows lack of proportionality between zero and the typical 60 percent to 70 percent passing score. As Heflebower et al. (2014) stated, "The traditional grading practice of using a zero to indicate incomplete work is antithetical to standards-based grading" (p. 59). Additionally, zeros typically don't help to create student responsibility and may, in fact, demotivate the very students teachers assumed they would help. Rather, students may receive a *no mark* (NM) or *incomplete* (I) to indicate missing work. This still conveys that a student needs to complete the assessment yet avoids the detrimental effect that assigning and averaging an automatic zero may have on a student's summative grade. See Heflebower et al. (2014) for more information.

Many teachers who implement standards-based learning are concerned about avoiding zeros when students do not complete work. They believe their students will not do the work if they are not concerned about receiving a zero. In fact, it is our observation that students are more likely to complete the work in a standards-based learning environment because of their involvement with their learning progression on the standards. Students want to receive feedback on this learning progression, and this is a strong motivator. Another way to consider the issue is whether you want to develop students who complete work from internal self-motivation or from the threat of a consequence. Most educators would agree that student self-motivation is preferable, and standards-based learning helps develop that.

Knowing the Limitations of Averaging

Knowing the limitations of averaging relates to the use of zeros, yet it implies that teachers are weighting earlier performances equally to those later in the learning of a particular prioritized standard or topic and applying a pure average to calculate a summative grade. Averaging while weighting sections differently may lessen this issue, yet the concept is to be mindful of whether calculations of central tendency are best indicators of the achievement information students provide.

Figure 4.7 shows the effect of three different measures of central tendency in a traditional grading format: (1) mean, (2) median, and (3) mode. It then adds the inclusion of a zero into the grading mix and shows the effect it has on a student's grade.

Mean (Average)	Median (Central Value)	Mode (Most Occurring)
80	80	80
83	83	83
85	85	85
92	92	92
75	75	75
85	85	85
90	90	90
Mean = 84.2	Median = 85	Mode = 85
Adding a 0	**Adding a 0**	**Adding a 0**
Mean = 73.75	Median = 84	Mode = 85

Figure 4.7: Traditional grading using central tendency and adding a zero.

In a standards-based system, while a zero might be used as a place holder (although we recommend other notation, as mentioned previously), it will not completely wreck a student's grade. It will show that the student has not yet completed that assessment. Additionally, when used with a series of scores from other assessments, the zero does not artificially lower the student's grade. Consider the series of scores in figure 4.8 using a standards-based approach. The student has missed a quiz and currently has a zero holding that place; however, since the teacher is considering the entire body of evidence and using the standards-based concepts of mounting evidence and IRT, the zero does not negatively affect the student's summative score. In fact, in this scenario, once the teacher sees evidence of the student's ability to handle the content on other assessments, the student may not even need to take the assessment he or she missed.

Prioritized standard: Types of business ownership					
Student Name	Preassessment	Quiz	Mid-Unit Quiz	Test	Summative Grade
Madie	2.0	0	3.0	3.0	3.0

Figure 4.8: Zero as a placeholder in a standards-based approach.

Separating What Students Know From How They Behave

Separating what students know from how they behave is an important point in a standards-learning environment. We certainly appreciate the importance of behavioral skills (participating, meeting deadlines, following direction, and the like), and we converge with the thinking of many others (Guskey & Bailey, 2001; Moss & Brookhart, 2009) to consider these skills separately. Therefore, teachers should aim to provide students with two summative grades based on proficiency scales: one for academic knowledge and skills, the other for related behaviors. Figure 4.9 displays a proficiency scale for behavioral skills that teachers in Monett, Missouri, created and used consistently in their schools.

Figure 4.10 (page 92) shows an example of a scale for one specific life skill: work completion (for additional details on this concept, see Marzano & Haystead, 2008). This scale assists teachers in clearly defining their expectations for this life skill, and at the same time allows students to assess their own performance on this skill. We will address this topic more in chapter 6 (page 121), when we discuss the need to report life skills separate from academic knowledge and skills.

Using a consistent behavioral scale allows for teachers to provide a summative grade to students about their behaviors. As mathematics teacher Patricia L. Scriffiny (2008) stated, "The system must not allow students to mask their level of understanding with their attendance, their level of effort, or other peripheral issues" (p. 72). Combining behavioral and academic skills often results in inaccurate summative grades. As Heflebower et al. (2014) stated, "The traditional practice of combining academic and nonacademic factors can inflate or deflate a student's grade, producing a number that means different things to different students, parents, and teachers" (p. 64).

Respectful			
1 **Rarely Meets Expectations**	**2** **Occasionally Meets Expectations**	**3** **Consistently Meets Expectations**	**4** **Consistently Exceeds Expectations**
Possible indicators of being respectful:			
Exhibits a positive attitude			
Contributes to the positive flow in class			
Respects self, others, and property			
Follows basic classroom instructions			
Responsible			
1 **Rarely Meets Expectations**	**2** **Occasionally Meets Expectations**	**3** **Consistently Meets Expectations**	**4** **Consistently Exceeds Expectations**
Possible indicators of being responsible:			
Arrives to class prepared			
Has a strong work ethic			
Consistently turns in assignments			
Attends regularly			
Makes up work in a timely manner			
Learner			
1 **Rarely Meets Expectations**	**2** **Occasionally Meets Expectations**	**3** **Consistently Meets Expectations**	**4** **Consistently Exceeds Expectations**
Possible indicators of being an appropriate learner:			
Takes an active role in class activities			
Seeks clarification as needed			

Source: Adapted from © 2016–2017 by Michael Evans and colleagues. Used with permission.

Figure 4.9: Proficiency scale for behaviors.

Visit **MarzanoResources.com/reproducibles** for a free reproducible version of this figure.

Work Completion Proficiency Scale		
Level 4.0	In addition to level 3.0 performance, the student turns in assignments ahead of schedule and with correct formatting.	
	Level 3.5	In addition to level 3.0 performance, the student shows partial success at level 4.0.
Level 3.0	The student will: • Meet all assignment deadlines • Turn in assignments that meet all requirements and formats	
	Level 2.5	The student is successful with level 2.0 elements and partially successful with level 3.0 elements.
Level 2.0	The student is successful with the simpler details and behaviors such as: • Turns in a majority of assignments on time, but not all • Turns in assignments that meet some of the formatting requirements	
	Level 1.5	The student is partially successful with level 2.0 elements without prompting.
Level 1.0	With prompting, the student is partially successful with level 2.0 elements.	
	Level 0.5	With help or prompting, the student is partially successful with level 2.0 elements.

Source: Adapted from Marzano & Haystead, 2008.

Figure 4.10: Work completion proficiency scale.

Acknowledging Unique Considerations Among Elementary and Secondary Schools

Acknowledging unique considerations among elementary and secondary schools means just that. As teachers consider figuring summative grades for students, the levels they teach have differing needs and concerns about grades. For instance, many elementary schools already report out grades using a connection to local or state (or province) standards. In fact, many also separate academic achievement from behavioral performance. Yet, as students progress through the educational system, the needs and emphasis about summative grades may change.

At the secondary level, grades tend to have more external importance. Colleges and universities use them for entrance, and scholarship committees and even specific secondary awards like valedictorian or salutatorian honors use them. Therefore, as teachers reflect on their grading practices and consider student needs, we suggest a thorough and thoughtful plan and discussion about these ideas. In fact, Heflebower et al. (2014) suggested using a set of questions as teachers reflect on their own grading practices and philosophies:

- What is the definition of a grade?
- Why do we grade?

- What should a grade represent?
- What role should homework, attendance, behavior, and participation play in grading?
- What role should re-testing play in grading?
- Is grading fair and equitable in your classes? Why? (p. 102)

These questions can serve individual teachers, teacher collaborative teams, or whole departments, as well as an entire school staff. The results may guide the various aspects of grading to be celebrated or challenged. For example, a celebration might be that all teachers within a school are in favor of the use of retesting as a part of their grading practice. This immediately establishes a covenant among the staff that they can build on as grading practices are addressed schoolwide.

Unusual Patterns of Performance

Sometimes unusual, or aberrant, patterns of scores emerge that indicate learners might be moving up and down between levels in their learning (Marzano, 2006). For example, a pattern of scores might look like: 2.0, 2.5, 3.0, 2.5, 3.0. In these situations, the patterns are not necessarily a clear linear pattern of growth. However, teachers can still apply the concept of mounting evidence based on the specific situation. It is important to keep in mind that the summative grade represents a collection and monitoring of scores. The examples in figures 4.11 and 4.12 demonstrate how a teacher might handle different types of scoring patterns.

Prioritized standard: Types of business ownership						
Student Name	Preassessment	Quiz	Mid-Unit Quiz	Test	Quiz	Summative Grade
Madie	2.0	2.5	3.0	2.5	3.0	3.0

Source: Marzano, 2006.

Figure 4.11: Example of an unusual pattern of assessment scores.

Prioritized standard: Types of business ownership						
Student Name	Preassessment	Quiz	Mid-Unit Quiz	Test	Quiz	Summative Grade
Madie	2.0	2.0	3.0	3.0	2.5	3.0

Source: Marzano, 2006.

Figure 4.12: Additional example of an unusual pattern of assessment scores.

Consider the score pattern in figure 4.11: 2.0, 2.5, 3.0, 2.5, 3.0. In reviewing the fourth score, 2.5, the teacher knows the student successfully demonstrated level 3.0 knowledge prior to that assessment and successfully again after that assessment. In this case, the teacher could meet with the student and use a quick conversation to reconcile what the student did incorrectly and determine if she understood the concept clearly. If this conversation verifies the student has the level 3.0 knowledge or skills, then it is accurate to infer a summative score of 3.0.

The pattern in figure 4.12 (page 93) indicates the student's most recent assessment was lower than two prior assessments: 2.0, 2.0, 3.0, 3.0, 2.5. The teacher has evidence from two prior assessments that indicates this student can perform at the 3.0 level, and the quiz score may simply be a case of the student not having her best day during that assessment. In this situation, the teacher has other viable options he or she can use to help clarify the student's level of learning. One option would be for the teacher to have a probing conversation with the student to determine the level of knowledge and the reasons for the drop in performance on the most recent assessment. Another option would be to offer the student an additional assessment opportunity to demonstrate her level of knowledge. The additional assessment opportunity could reassess what the student missed or it could involve a complete reassessment of the entire content. That decision is up to the teacher based on knowledge of the individual student and situation.

Another situation that may arise is that a class, or a majority of students in the class, suddenly demonstrates a loss of performance on one assessment after demonstrating strong performance on prior assessments. When large numbers of students experience this pattern of performance, the teacher is wise to examine the assessment before discussing the performance with his or her students. It may be that the assessment items do not properly align with the levels of the proficiency scale, or there may be another problem with the assessment such as bias or a confusing format. Usually, when there is a problem with performance across most of the students, the problem lies in the assessment rather than students.

When dealing with illogical or unusual patterns of performance, the concept of mounting evidence still applies. Basically, a teacher uses a variety of informational sources from any one of the three types of assessment information (obtrusive, unobtrusive, or student-generated) to conclude a student's level of understanding on a proficiency scale. The true score is basically a score that counters the effects of random error inherent within all assessments. It is likely the most accurate indication of a student's performance, and it is determined by replications of measurements that cancel out the error over time (Marzano, 2018). To further this idea, Marzano (2018) suggested asking two questions:

> First, if the student's true score is 3.0, how likely is it that he or she would exhibit this pattern? . . . If the student's true score is lower than 3.0, how likely is it that he or she would exhibit this pattern? (p. 74)

Extra Credit and Retakes

In a traditional classroom, extra credit is a method by which students can do additional work to assist in raising their grades and to recover from poor grades as a result of the effects of mixing behavior (participation and turning in work late) with academic performance. In a standards-based classroom, each score measuring student performance aligns to one or more priority standards. Assessment of student performance takes on a very different approach, with the scores recorded indicating student progress toward proficiency on the standards. It may often be the case that some students do more assessments than other students. In the case of standards-based scores, students do not receive credit or points in the gradebook. In such an environment, the entire notion of extra credit does not make sense. If a student needs the opportunity to show growth on a standard beyond assessments given to the rest of the class, there is no reason not to provide these additional performance opportunities. Standards-based learning advocates for students having multiple opportunities and methods to demonstrate proficiency on the standards, and thus the number of assessments can vary depending on the needs of particular students. Additional opportunities to perform are in no way *extra*, in the sense of extra credit. They are simply part of standard operating procedure in a standards-based classroom.

Several concerns may emerge for a teacher anticipating adopting such a policy. First, it will appear that multiple opportunities to demonstrate proficiency will create an enormous workload for the teacher in the form of scoring these additional assessments. Second, teachers may wonder why a student who knows he or she will have multiple additional opportunities to show proficiency will attempt to reach proficiency on the first or second try. Finally, teachers sometimes wonder if giving multiple opportunities to a student in need of them, beyond what is necessary for other students in the class, is fair to those other students.

Although it is true that teachers will need to create additional assessments to provide students with multiple opportunities, this is only a concern in the first few years in which a teacher instructs in a standards-based classroom. Rapidly, teachers create *banks* of assessments that can serve them throughout subsequent years. The more immediate concern may be the workload of scoring these additional assessments. If students know they can retake an assessment, haven't we removed the incentive to try the first or even the second time?

Teachers who teach in a standards-based classroom often find that these concerns never really emerge. Students who focus on growth along a learning progression, particularly if they have set and are monitoring their own progress toward personal goals aligned to those standards, are eager to see if their performance is improving. Teachers often find that homework completion rates improve when students are monitoring their own progress, and the same principle applies to assessments. Students will often try hard the first time to achieve proficiency.

But retakes do mean additional scoring, and that means an increased workload for the teacher. How can teachers in a standards-based learning environment minimize this? Although it is a core principle of standards-based learning that students receive multiple opportunities to demonstrate proficiency, it is not true that such opportunities should be automatic. Thus, teachers often apply a system whereby students must qualify to do a retake. Teachers can require that students do additional work in preparation for retakes. In fact, asking students what they have done that will improve their performance next time sends the message that it is important to prepare for the initial assessments, so as to avoid additional work. Students quickly understand this concept, which reduces the volume of retakes.

In offering many opportunities to some students, when other students have already reached proficiency and don't need those opportunities, might seem unfair. But it should be noted that fair does not mean equal. What is fair for some students is not the same for all. Although these ideas sometimes puzzle teachers, most students inherently understand this concept. If a student is struggling to understand some knowledge or perform a skill, it doesn't seem unreasonable that the student should be able to keep trying. At the same time, a student who achieves proficiency consistently does not need to continue to demonstrate that proficiency simply because other students in the class need additional opportunities. Teachers are simply adjusting the assessment system to the individual needs of students. We would not be concerned with the fairness question if a special-needs student required additional opportunities. The question is really the same for all students. Not every student learns in the same way or at the same pace.

Summary

A combination of three different types of assessment—(1) obtrusive, (2) unobtrusive, and (3) student generated—is likely to provide several varied data points of student performance. After teachers align these assessments and their correlating assignments with proficiency scales using item response theory, they then have scores that better reflect what students know and are able to do. This chapter highlighted a number of considerations for assistance in figuring scores into summative grades more accurately. It proposed that teachers glean information from a variety of scores and use those to determine a summative grade. When so doing, teachers should consider a few guidelines—including avoiding zeros, giving more weight to more recent scores, and separating students' behavior from their academics—to create a more valid and reliable means for concluding students' summative grades. Additionally, this chapter addressed concerns surrounding grades for extra credit and how to use retakes in a standards-based learning environment.

The following chapter will discuss special considerations for teaching exceptional students in a standards-based classroom.

Teaching Exceptional Students

Standards-based learning environments affect all students, yet they affect some—particularly students with disabilities, ELs, and gifted learners—a bit differently. It is important to address all types of learners when considering an effective standards-based learning environment. In so doing, teachers may need additional supports and guidance when working with some students, especially those who may need accommodations or modified instruction. We refer to these students as *exceptional students*.

As Heflebower et al. (2017) stated:

> One might argue that all students are unique and exceptional learners. Students learn in a variety of different ways and have a variety of strengths and talents. However, the United States has defined several distinct groups as exceptional for the purposes of schooling and education. These include students with disabilities, English learners, and gifted and talented students. (p. 71)

In this chapter, we explain how to use multitiered systems of support (MTSS) and proficiency scales—specifically presenting ideas for the instructional and assessment side of the scales—in order to support students classified as exceptional learners. We will then discuss necessary modifications and accommodations for students with disabilities, English learners, and gifted learners and explore grading in special classes: electives, AP, and IB.

Linking Standards-Based Learning and Multitiered Systems of Support

Proficiency scales can direct teachers' decisions regarding the level of support they need to provide exceptional students as well as how to grade them (Marzano, 2010). These levels of support are closely associated with behavior-inclusive MTSS, such as positive behavior interventions and supports (PBIS) and academic and behavioral support—response to intervention (RTI). George Batsche et al. (2005) defined MTSS as "the practice of providing high-quality instruction and interventions matched to student need, monitoring progress frequently to make decisions about changes in instruction or goals, and applying child response data to important educational decisions" (p. 9). Orla Higgins Averill and Claudia Rinaldi (2011) added, "MTSS leverages the principles of RTI and PBIS and integrates a continuum of system-wide resources, strategies, structures and practices" (p. 91). In standards-based learning systems, the collective work of prioritizing standards, creating and using proficiency scales, and aligning classroom assessments and grades is the systemic approach supporting MTSS efforts. Such a system provides clarity of critical content, differentiated instruction, and assessment to meet the needs of all students so all can achieve higher levels of academic and behavioral success.

Some teachers refer to the academic side of MTSS as Tiers 1, 2, and 3. As stated earlier, Tier 1 comprises schoolwide efforts of high-quality initial core instruction. Focusing on high-quality initial instruction increases the likelihood of the vast majority of students reaching proficiency on prioritized standards. As Heflebower et al. (2017) said, "When initial instruction is thoughtful, well-planned, and aligned to the knowledge and skills in the academic standards, students are more likely to achieve proficiency the first time" (p. 62). Tiers 2 and 3 provide increasingly more intensive individualized instructional supports and interventions (Batsche et al., 2005). As teachers take into account all levels of MTSS, they are simultaneously addressing standards-based learning, and vice versa. When teachers clarify the prioritized standards, they are helping set clear Tier 1 targets for all students. As teachers plan for exceptional learners, they are addressing Tiers 2 and 3. Typically, Tier 2 supports will assist learners who need some accommodations to their initial learning efforts. We address this later in this chapter as we consider using proficiency scales with students needing more support or extensions. As teachers work toward Tier 3 interventions per students' needs, they may consider more modified scales and grading practices. As this chapter unfolds, teachers will see the direct connections between the tiers of MTSS and standards-based learning.

Using Proficiency Scales With Exceptional Learners

The majority of students will be able to efficiently use the general education proficiency scales we discussed in chapter 1 (page 7). However, some students will require teachers to make accommodations or modifications to proficiency scales. Accommodations are supports put in place to help students achieve grade-level expectations. They do not change the level of the expectations for students. *Accommodations* simply allow students to demonstrate their proficiency in a manner that is best for them. They do not result in lower or higher expectations, and they do not require a different grading system. An example often used is that of wearing glasses. This is an accommodation, but most of us wouldn't think of lowering expectations or a grade because an individual wears glasses. The expectations remain the same. *Modifications*, on the other hand, *do* change the level of expectations for students. Modifications shift the expectations either up or down from the grade-level expectancies. For example, expectations for students at 2.0 *might* become the 3.0 expectations for a student with modifications. In other words, the proficiency scale content slides up (or down) as needed for students requiring such modifications.

The following figure illustrates one way to incorporate appropriate supports—either modifications or accommodations (figure 5.1).

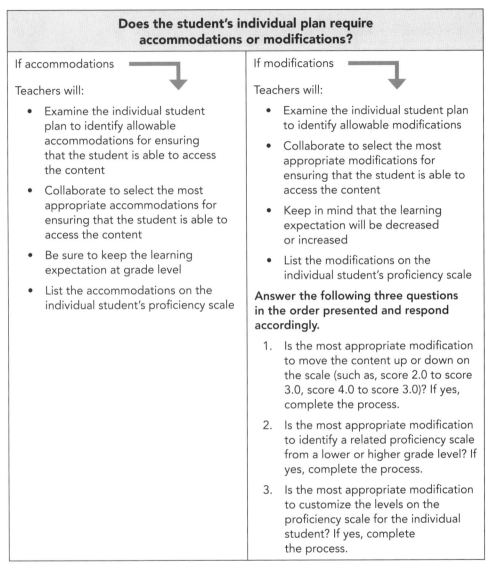

Figure 5.1: Illustration of accommodations and modifications.

As figure 5.1 depicts, the teacher first asks, "Does this student need accommodations or modifications on this prioritized standard?" If the answer is no, the teacher uses the general education proficiency scale created for the course or grade level. If, however, the teacher responds that a student *will* require supports, the next questions begets, "Would an accommodation be enough, or is a modification required?" If the teacher is uncertain, it is always advisable to reference the student's individualized educational plan (IEP), the legal document that the support team creates (often the classroom teacher, special education teacher, or multidisciplinary team) to direct such support. As noted on the left side of figure 5.1 (page 99), and employing the concept of *least restrictive environment*, the teacher would first want to use accommodations that may help.

A preassessment (see Administering the Preassessment, page 36) is one way to identify students who may need accommodations or modifications. Teachers should base each preassessment on the proficiency scales they are using in a course or grade level and contain items for the 2.0, 3.0, and 4.0 levels of the scale. Since instruction for the content on a preassessment does not occur until after teachers administer a preassessment, it is likely that most students will fall short of the score 3.0 level. Students with disabilities and ELs may score even lower. Thus, these students will likely need extra support and scaffolding to achieve the 3.0 level. However, a gifted learner may score at the 3.0 level or higher, indicating that he or she should pursue more complex activities while the rest of the students experience the planned instruction.

After determining students' baselines, teachers are better equipped to create proficiency scales with modifications or accommodations to guide these differentiated learning experiences. To create such a proficiency scale, teachers should begin with the general education proficiency scale, and use that as the basis.

When combining accommodations and a proficiency scale, oftentimes a common set of accommodations may be beneficial to students. These may include, but are not limited to, the following seven general items (Heflebower et al., 2014).

1. Offering more time

2. Providing more space

3. Using voice-to-text software

4. Seating the student away from distractions

5. Allowing for different modes of teaching (auditory explanations, pictures, and so on)

6. Using graphic organizers

7. Increasing font size

The most important requirement of an accommodation is that it does *not* change the expectation of proficiency on the prioritized standard. This is important! If a student has too much support when unnecessary, the accommodation may actually inhibit growth and confidence later on. Use only what is needed, when it is needed.

Teachers should document accommodations for specific students on the right side of a proficiency scale (see figure 5.2). In the example, the text in parentheses indicates accommodations that might be made as students demonstrate their knowledge and skill.

Prioritized standard: The student will apply knowledge of organizational patterns found in informational text.

Level	Description	Sample Activities (With Accommodations)
4.0	In addition to score 3.0 performance, the student demonstrates in-depth inferences and applications that go beyond what was taught.	When the teacher provides the student with a folder containing an informational text (of no more than four paragraphs) cut into paragraphs, the student reads (or listens to) and organizes the text. The student then identifies (from a list of possible structures) the structure the author uses (for example, main idea with supporting detail, sequence, compare and contrast, fact and opinion) and cites specific examples within the text that are characteristic of the identified organizational structure. The student writes (or dictates) an original text that incorporates a self-selected organizational pattern.
3.0	The student will apply knowledge of organizational patterns found in informational text, such as: • Sequence • Cause and effect • Compare and contrast • Fact and opinion • Description • Proposition and support	When the teacher provides the student with a folder containing an informational text (of no more than three paragraphs) cut into paragraphs, the student reads (or listens to) and organizes the text, then identifies (from a list of possible structures) the structure the author uses (for example, main idea with supporting detail, sequence, compare and contrast, fact and opinion). The student classifies short selections of text using a graphic organizer (texts may be read to the student).
2.0	The student will: • Sequence three or more events in informational text • Identify the cause and effect in a given text • Identify what is being compared and contrasted in a given text • Recognize or recall specific vocabulary, such as *sequence, cause, effect, compare, contrast, proposition, description,* and *support*	The student reads (or listens to) a text and highlights signal words within the text that indicate the structure of the text (for example, *first, second,* and *third* signal chronology; *because* or *as a result of* signal cause and effect; *above, beneath,* and *beside* signal description). The student identifies (three) types of texts (for example, biography, article, or story) and the organizational patterns usually associated with those types of texts. The student defines specific terms associated with organizational patterns by matching terms from a word bank to provided definitions.

Source: Adapted from Heflebower et al., 2014, p. 76.

Figure 5.2: Sample proficiency scale with accommodations.

Some students will need additional supports to the accommodations teachers already provide. These situations warrant modifications to the expectations. As the right side of figure 5.1 illustrates (page 99), modifications will *change* the nature of the expectations a teacher has for a student. Modifications should only be made for a student whose IEP specifies such changes are necessary. As Heflebower et al. (2014) noted:

> When modifications are made for students, their grades show progress toward their *modified* prioritized standards, which are different (simpler or more complex) than those of the general student population. The expectations are no longer the same. While modifications apply to only a small number of students, it is important for educators to understand that modifications change the descriptors on the left side of the scale (and therefore what students' grades mean) in addition to the example activities on the right side of the scale. (p. 80)

Again, as the IEP dictates, use the modifications required and consider the following three questions.

1. Is the most appropriate modification to move the content up or down on the scale (such as, score 2.0 to score 3.0, score 4.0 to score 3.0)? If yes, complete the process.

2. Is the most appropriate modification to identify a related proficiency scale from a lower or higher grade level? If yes, complete the process.

3. Is the most appropriate modification to customize the levels on the proficiency scale for the individual student? If yes, complete the process.

It is also notable to consider scaffolding for students *initially* not ready for grade-level content. For example, if a grade 8 student is reading at the sixth-grade level, his or her teacher may use modified supports initially. However, as the student grows more confident in using support strategies (for example, read-check-summarize), teachers should support the student in moving toward grade-level content prior to the culmination of the year, and likely prior to asking the student to take grade-level external assessments (such as statewide assessments or district benchmarks). In virtually all assessments requiring reading, teachers expect a student to read grade-level passages.

The following sections describe specific accommodations and modifications that teachers may make to proficiency scales for students with disabilities, ELs, and gifted learners.

Students With Disabilities

Creating a modified scale involves adjusting the prioritized standard at the 3.0 level and the simpler goal at the 2.0 level, as well as the sample assessment activities for levels 2.0, 3.0, and 4.0. Sample modifications include shortening requirements or assignments and varying reading levels for independent reading. Some options for modifying scales for students with disabilities include:

- Moving the level descriptors up on the scale, so that score 2.0 descriptors become score 3.0 descriptors and score 3.0 descriptors become score 4.0 descriptors

- Changing the sample activities on the scale to make them simpler

- Inserting descriptors from lower-grade-level scales

See figure 5.3 for a scale modified for students with disabilities.

General education prioritized standard: The student will apply knowledge of organizational patterns found in informational text.		
Modified prioritized standard: The student will identify organizational patterns found in informational text.		
4.0	In addition to score 3.0 performance, the student demonstrates in-depth inferences and applications that go beyond what was taught.	The student identifies the sequence of events in an informational text. For example, after being read a text about the life of Abraham Lincoln, the student correctly restates the events in order. The student describes a cause-and-effect or compare-and-contrast pattern in an informational text. The student identifies statements that are fact and statements that are opinion. For example, given two sentences (such as *October is a month* versus *October is the best month*), the student correctly identifies which is a fact and which is an opinion.
3.0	The student will identify organizational patterns found in informational text, such as sequence, cause and effect, and compare and contrast.	The student identifies the sequence of events in an informational text. For example, after listening to a text about the life of Abraham Lincoln, the student correctly sequences pictures from the text. Or, after listening to a text about tornadoes, the student determines what happens after the air begins to rotate. The student identifies the cause and effect described in an informational text. For example, after listening to a text about smoking, the student states, "Smoking cigarettes can cause coughing, cancer, yellowing of teeth, and bad breath." The student identifies a compare-and-contrast organizational pattern. For example, a student can explain how a dog is like and unlike a cat after listening to the following sentences: "The dog, like a cat, makes a good pet. Unlike a cat, a dog likes to hide bones by burying them."

Figure 5.3: Grade 7 ELA scale with modifications for students with disabilities.   Continued →

| 2.0 | The student will:

 • Sequence three or more events in informational text

 • Identify the cause of an event

 • Identify a comparison in informational text

 • Recognize or recall specific terminology, such as *order*, *sequence*, *cause*, *compare*, and *alike* | When given a series of three pictures, the student identifies which one happened first, next, and last after listening to a story or informational text.

 After listening to a short informational text, the student identifies what happened first, next, and last.

 The student identifies the cause of an event based on a text. For example, "Icy roads are the cause of many automobile accidents."

 The student identifies comparisons in an informational text, such as "Nebraska is a neighbor to South Dakota, Iowa, Kansas, and Colorado. Nebraska is larger than Iowa." |

Source: Heflebower et al., 2014, p. 81.

This scale (figure 5.3, page 103), based on an IEP, features a prioritized standard that is less complex than the one for general education students.

For a description of possible accommodations for students with disabilities, see Using Proficiency Scales With Exceptional Learners (page 98).

English Learners

Like those for students with disabilities, teachers should document accommodations that they provide ELs on students' individual proficiency scales. Common examples of accommodations for ELs include the following.

- Showing examples of a completed assignment to model the correct format

- Writing assignments and directions on the board in both print and cursive

- Providing a bilingual assistant or interpreter to explain concepts in the students' primary language

- Providing manipulatives to help students complete certain tasks

- Rewriting story problems using short sentences, pictures, and illustrations to support understanding

- Teaching related vocabulary using pictures, visuals, and multimedia

- Providing reading materials at the instructional level of the student

- Providing audio recordings for the learner

- Providing adequate background information for the learner

- Teaching reading strategies that enable ELs to predict, connect, question, and visualize a story

Educators should adjust only the right column of the proficiency scale to reflect the accommodations they are providing; these adjustments should be personalized to meet the ELs' specific instructional needs. Once again, the learning expectations are the same for ELs and general education students, but ELs require different supports to demonstrate their competence.

Modifications for ELs involve changing both the descriptors and the sample assessment activities on the proficiency scale. Common modifications for ELs include lowering the reading or difficulty level of texts, shortening assignments, using supplementary materials, allowing computer or word processor assistance, and modifying activities and assessments.

While ELs may require modified instruction and expectations for mastery, the ultimate goal is for these students to eventually reach the same score 3.0 level as general education students. Consequently, we advise modifying scales for ELs by moving the prioritized standard to the 4.0 level. The 2.0 goal then becomes the 3.0 goal, and new 2.0 expectations arise. This approach keeps the learning target on the proficiency scale, yet ensures the expectations for the learner are more appropriate for the individual student.

See figure 5.4 to view a scale modified for an EL.

General education prioritized standard: The student will apply knowledge of organizational patterns found in informational text.		
Modified prioritized standard: The student will apply knowledge of organizational patterns found in informational text.		
4.0	The student will apply knowledge of organizational patterns found in informational text, such as: • Sequence • Cause and effect • Compare and contrast • Fact and opinion • Description • Proposition and support	When the teacher provides the student with a folder containing an informational text (of no more than three paragraphs) cut into paragraphs, and the text is read to the student or translated into the student's native language, the student reads (or listens to) and organizes the text. The student then identifies the structure the author uses (for example, main idea with supporting detail, sequence, compare and contrast, fact and opinion). The student listens to a short informational text in his or her native language and draws pictures in a graphic organizer to represent key events. The student uses the pictures to retell the sequence of events in the text.

Figure 5.4: Grade 7 ELA scale with modifications for English learners.

Continued →

| 3.0 | The student will:

 • Sequence three or more events in informational text
 • Identify the cause and effect presented in a given text
 • Identify what is being compared and contrasted in a given text
 • Recognize or recall specific vocabulary, such as *sequence*, *cause*, *effect*, *compare*, *contrast*, *proposition*, and *support* | The student listens to a short informational text in his or her native language and arranges pictures of events from the text in the order that they happened in the text.

 The student reads an adaptive text aloud to a teacher and highlights the signal words within the text that indicate the structure of the text (for example, *first*, *second*, and *third* signal chronology; *because* and *as a result of* signal cause and effect; *above*, *beneath*, and *beside* signal description).

 With the support of a translator, the student identifies different types of text and the type of organizational pattern often associated with the type of text (for example, biography often uses a sequence of events; editorials are often proposition and support).

 The student matches terms associated with organizational patterns from a word bank to provided definitions (presented pictorially or in the student's native language). |
| 2.0 | The student will:

 • Identify the organizational pattern of sequence found in an informational text | The student listens to two short pieces of informational text. The teacher asks the student which piece of text uses the organizational pattern of sequence. The student identifies which text follows this pattern. |

Source: Heflebower et al., 2014, p. 83.

In order to support the student, some of the assessment activities ask the student to read or listen in his or her native language. However, the major difference between this scale and the general education scale is that the level of thinking on this scale is lower. The type and length of text the teacher asks the student to engage with represent this.

Gifted Learners

Gifted learners also require accommodations that teachers should document on individual proficiency scales, as many may attain goals sooner than general education students. Accommodation activities for gifted learners include:

• Grouping students with other gifted students or higher-level learners

• Adjusting instruction to include advanced processes, products, and assessments

• Using thematic, project-based, and problem-based instruction to connect learning across the curriculum

- Allowing students to choose how to approach a problem or assignment

- Providing students the opportunity to design their own learning opportunities in areas of strength, interest, and passion

- Inviting students to explore different points of view on a topic of study and compare them

- Providing learning centers where students are in charge of their learning

- Asking students higher-level questions that foster critical thinking

- Requiring students to consider causes, experiences, and facts to draw a conclusion or make connections to other areas of learning

- Allowing students to demonstrate mastery of a concept right away rather than engaging in unnecessary skill practice

Teachers should refrain from grouping gifted students with students from lower levels for remediation purposes and from asking gifted learners to simply complete more work than other students because they feel that it isn't the gifted students' responsibility to teach the lower-achieving students. However, using this strategy periodically may help strengthen the learning for the gifted learner. Likewise, asking students to simply complete more of the same level of work is not addressing their greater needs. Rather, it is important for practice work and assessments to delve deeper with thinking, problem solving, or inquiry for gifted students. This way, the teacher is not simply providing an accumulation of more work but rather offering these students different challenges that will extend their minds and deepen their understanding.

Gifted students work toward the same prioritized standard as general education students, but the teacher personalizes the right column of each gifted student's scale by adjusting the activity's description or raising the level of independence the student needs to perform tasks. Regardless of the methodology teachers use to generate the activities, it is important to remember that the expectations (prioritized standards) are the same for all students.

Modifications may also be necessary for gifted learners. These modifications might involve:

- Making learning targets more difficult

- Requiring students to apply their knowledge in unique, real-world situations

- Rephrasing prioritized standards as reflective guiding questions

- Requiring students to create hypotheses, ask questions, and analyze their learning

Modified scales for gifted students increase the rigor and complexity of the expectations for each level of the scale. One way to do this is to shift the expectations downward: score 3.0 expectations become score 2.0 expectations, and score 4.0 expectations become score 3.0 expectations. Teachers then create new 4.0 expectations. Another way is to create a new, more complex 3.0 goal and to adjust the 2.0 and 4.0 goals accordingly. Yet another method involves requiring gifted students to achieve 4.0 level expectations rather than 3.0 expectations. Sample assessment tasks require students to extend their thinking through the development of products that demonstrate higher levels of thinking. See figure 5.5 to view a scale modified for a gifted student. The proficiency scale there has more complex expectations than the general education scale, as the expectations have shifted.

Once teachers modify their proficiency scales for exceptional students, they must assign them a grade. This grading methodology also has special considerations pertaining to exceptional students. We will discuss these in the following section.

Assigning Grades to Exceptional Students

To determine grades for exceptional students, teachers should follow the same guidelines chapter 4 (page 71) described. These include:

- Examining the student's performance on assignments and assessments (mounting evidence)

- Giving more weight to recent information (if necessary, discussing the content with the student to shed light on his or her learning progress)

- Limiting the use of zeros

- Knowing the limitations of averaging

- Separating what students know from how they behave

- Acknowledging unique considerations among elementary and secondary schools

However, teachers should use the exceptional student's individualized proficiency scale during grading. For example, a teacher assigning a grade to a student with disabilities would assign scores to students based on how closely their performance matches the levels and descriptors on their unique proficiency scales. The following story discusses a teacher who modified proficiency scales for gifted students (Heflebower et al., 2014).

General education prioritized standard: The student will apply knowledge of organizational patterns found in informational text.

Modified prioritized standard: The student will compare and contrast the structures of texts and analyze their structures in detail to understand the role of particular sentences in developing and refining a key concept and to understand how each text's structure contributes to its meaning and style.

4.0	In addition to score 3.0 performance, the student demonstrates in-depth inferences and applications that go beyond what was taught.	The student listens to a song (for example, "Scenes From an Italian Restaurant" by Billy Joel) and describes its structure using standard terminology (for example, use plot terminology such as *exposition*, *rising action*, *climax*, *falling action*, and *resolution* to describe the flashback in the Billy Joel song).
3.0	The student will: • Compare and contrast the structure of two or more grade-appropriate texts and analyze how the differing structure of each text contributes to its meaning and style • Analyze in detail the structure of a specific paragraph in a grade-appropriate text, including the role of particular sentences in developing and refining a key concept	The student compares and contrasts several texts (for example, "O Captain! My Captain!" by Walt Whitman or an excerpt from Russell Freedman's *Lincoln: A Photobiography* or Seymour Reit's *Behind Rebel Lines*) and then participates in a discussion where he or she explains the purpose and the value of the structures in the texts.
2.0	The student will: • Recognize or recall specific vocabulary, such as *analyze*, *compare*, *concept*, *contrast*, *detail*, *develop*, *meaning*, *paragraph*, *refine*, *role*, *sentence*, *structure*, and *style* • Describe the general structure of a specific paragraph in a grade-appropriate text • Identify the general structure of a specific grade-appropriate text • Recognize signal words or phrases associated with text structure (for example, *following*, *compared with*, *therefore*, *as a result of*) in a grade-appropriate text	The student reads a paragraph of informational text and then identifies and describes the organizational pattern used in the text. The student sorts words and phrases that signal text structures and explains what the structures communicate about how to read and understand the text.

Source: Adapted from Heflebower et al., 2014, p. 84.

Figure 5.5: Grade 7 ELA scale with modifications for gifted learners.

When Ms. Janedis, a fourth-grade teacher, worked with students for whom she'd modified expectations for gifted learners, she wanted to be certain she recorded those expectations on the reporting document. As a result, Ms. Janedis worked with other teachers of gifted learners, curriculum specialists, and her administrators to devise a more meaningful way to communicate these differences. Because many of her gifted students were actually working on elements of the fifth-grade standards, she electronically pulled in all or part of the description of those fifth-grade standards and their corresponding proficiency scales. She then communicated this with the parents of gifted students who were receiving this modification during their individual learning plan conferences. Ms. Janedis explained that those advanced standards and components of standards would be printed directly onto the report cards. She would indicate, with an asterisk, those standards that were beyond the fourth-grade standards and note the grade level of the standards. This meant that a student may not receive all 3.0 or 4.0 designations if, in fact, the standards were advanced and the student had only mastered some to a 2.0 level. However, this practice would clearly help the student, parents, and teachers better align the classroom practices and expectations with the reporting document.

Grading practices for exceptional students can often feel unreliable. Teachers, students, and parents cannot always be sure that grades accurately reflect student learning. In order to address this issue, schools can put into place a system of clear prioritized standards organized into proficiency scales that articulate competencies and example of activities at each level. Students who perform at the 3.0 level have mastered the content. In the case of exceptional students, teachers can adapt the regular scales to reflect their educational needs. Using proficiency scales with accommodations or modifications can create a fair and consistent grading system that meets the needs of all students, including those with disabilities, ELs, and gifted learners.

Using Standards-Based Learning in Special Classes

Standards-based learning may apply in all courses students take; however, addressing standards-based learning in certain unique classes may present a distinct challenge. The following sections will discuss how to use standards-based learning with electives, Advanced Placement classes, and International Baccalaureate classes.

Standards-Based Learning and Electives

Just as standards are the basis for English language arts, mathematics, science, and social studies, they are provided for almost all non-core content areas as well. One of the challenges identified with standards for fine arts, physical education, technology, and other electives is that the standards are sometimes not as specific as they are for core content areas. For example, consider the following fine arts standard.

> The student will create, perform, exhibit, or participate in the arts.

While a team of art teachers may agree that this is a priority standard, it presents a challenge when it comes to developing proficiency scales and determining how to assess progress to the standard. Because of the difference in standards across content areas, it may be necessary for teachers of electives to approach scale development a bit differently than for core content areas.

We propose that teachers of elective courses may need to consider the following question when determining topics for proficiency scale development: *What is so important in this content area or course that it requires a proficiency scale?* The following vignette is an example of teachers responding to this question successfully.

The world language team of teachers at Victory High School are working collaboratively to develop proficiency scales for Spanish I, II, III, and IV. The standards upon which their curriculum processes are based are quite comprehensive and somewhat vague. They have decided to make decisions for proficiency scale development based on their professional judgment and expertise. Each proficiency scale will be a response to the question, "What is so important in Spanish I that it requires a proficiency scale?"

After doing a thorough examination of their standards, they have decided to develop five proficiency scales. The measurement topics of their scales are: (1) Interpersonal Communication, (2) Interpretive Communication, (3) Presentational Communication, (4) Cultural Perspectives, and (5) Grammar Topics. These scales will be used multiple times over the duration of Spanish I. Additionally, they are able to show standards alignment with each of their measurement topics.

While this team's approach to proficiency scale development is not based on priority standards, it allows for teachers to clearly communicate to students what they need to know and be able to do by the end of the course. It also allows them to ask students to set goals and track their progress. For example, consider the following scale example for the measurement topic of Grammar Topics (figure 5.6).

Score 4.0	The student will use the grammar topic in daily life communications.
Score 3.0	The student will use the grammar topic in context and conversation.
Score 2.0	The student will identify examples of the grammar topic (for example, greetings, food, commonly used words or phrases, or animals).
	The student will use the grammar topic in isolated examples.

Figure 5.6: Example scale for the measurement topic of Grammar Topics.

This scale allows for the teacher to give students the opportunity to determine their current level of performance on a specific grammar topic at any point in time. Let's say that the current grammar topic is greetings. A teacher may ask students to complete an exit activity at the end of a class period that responds to the prompt, "I believe I am currently at the _____ level on the proficiency scale because _____." One student response may be, "I believe I am currently at the score 2.0 level on the proficiency scale because I can list some examples of greetings, but I am not able to use them accurately yet." This reflection shows that the student understands he or she still has some learning to experience.

Another consideration for teachers of elective courses is the possible inclusion of rubrics to help determine a current level of performance. This consideration is necessary due to the lack of specificity of standards for some non-core content areas suggested earlier in this section. For example, when using the proficiency scale for Fundamentals of Art in figure 5.7, teachers might find a rubric to be very helpful for making decisions about current levels of performance.

Score 4.0	In addition to score 3.0, the student demonstrates in-depth inferences and applications that go beyond what was taught.
Score 3.0	The student demonstrates mastery of class-level skills and processes with no major errors or omissions.
Score 2.0	The student demonstrates mastery of all basic skills and processes and partial mastery of the higher-level skills and processes with no major errors or omissions.
Score 1.0	The student requires help to partially complete class-level skills and processes and some of the more complex ideas and processes.

Figure 5.7: Fundamentals of Art proficiency scale.

A rubric is needed to offer the details necessary related to any specific task the student is asked to complete. Suppose a seventh-grade classroom of students is working on drawing for a portion of a nine-week period. After providing the appropriate instruction, the teacher assigns a drawing task. Before asking students to complete the task, he or she overviews the scoring rubric that will be used to determine the quality of the drawing project. The following rubric (figure 5.8) is specific to the drawing task.

	Advanced	**Proficient**	**Basic**	**Beginning**
Craftsmanship	Artwork is impeccable and shows no evidence of smudge marks, rips, tears, or folds. No erasure lines showing.	Artwork is neat and shows very little evidence of smudge marks, rips, tears, or folds. A few erasure lines showing.	Artwork is somewhat messy and shows either smudge marks or rips, tears, or folds. Some erasure lines showing.	Artwork is messy and shows smudge marks and rips, tears, or folds. Erasure lines showing.

Techniques and Art Concepts	Artwork shows a mastery of advanced techniques in composition. All objects are placed in correct space. Negative and positive space is balanced. Paper is completely drawn on and shows a background, midground, and foreground.	Artwork shows good technique. All objects are placed in correct space. Negative and positive space is almost balanced. Paper is drawn on leaving some area undone and shows a background, midground, and foreground.	Artwork shows some technique and understanding of art concepts. Average use of negative and positive space. Paper is half filled and both foreground and background are clearly shown.	Artwork lacks technique or understanding of art concepts. Paper is left mainly blank, little area drawn on, and does not show a background, midground, or foreground.
Creativity	Artwork reflects a high level of originality. Student uses line, shading, or form in a highly original manner.	Artwork reflects originality. Student uses line, shading, or form in an original manner.	Artwork shows some evidence of originality. Student uses line, shading, or form in a slightly original manner.	Artwork shows little or no evidence of original thought. Student does not use line, shading, or form in a creative manner.
Shading and Proportion	Completed artwork is fully shaded showing excellent placement of light and darks using excellent drawing technique. Still life objects are in excellent proportion with real-life objects.	Completed artwork is almost fully shaded showing good placement of light and darks using good drawing technique. Still life objects are mostly in good proportion with real-life objects.	Completed artwork is half shaded showing average placement of light and darks using average drawing technique. Some still life objects are in proportion with real-life objects.	Completed artwork is not shaded or incorrectly shaded. Still life objects are incorrect in proportion with real-life objects.

Figure 5.8: Example drawing task rubric.

The student's performance on this rubric will be an indicator as to how the student is performing on the proficiency scale.

In summary, we believe all teachers should participate in prioritization and scale development processes. Having said this, it is important for teachers to consider the uniqueness of standards and to determine how to best approach curriculum and assessment practices for their content area or course. The end goal is for students to have clear understanding of what they need to know and be able to do, and for them to be able to monitor their own progress in an ongoing manner.

Standards-Based Learning and Advanced Placement Classes

AP classes provide a unique situation for the use of priority standards and proficiency scales. It may appear to some teachers that the intense nature of these classes and the dictated curriculum standards that College Board AP (2014) delineates in its course description guides would make the use of priority standards, proficiency scales, and the other elements of standards-based learning problematic. In fact, nothing could be further from the truth. AP classes are actually ideal situations for standards-based learning. Students are motivated to improve their knowledge and skills throughout the year and are provided specific feedback on the knowledge and skills through existing rubrics. College Board tests often make their learning journey in the class different than other, traditional methods of feedback and grading.

AP classes are in the unusual situation of serving two masters. While they, like all other classes in K–12 education, must hold to the state standards that each state's department of education provides, in most cases the class standards, based on College Board AP (2014) guidelines, far exceed the rigor of the state standards. Teachers of AP classes will want to make sure they are addressing every state standard for which they are responsible, but often the state standards will find their way to "supporting standard" status in an AP class. Teachers can create their AP class priority standards based on the AP course description. For example, in the case of AP English literature and composition, the AP course description includes information in the reading section:

> Reading in an AP course is both wide and deep. This reading necessarily builds upon and complements the reading done in previous English courses so that by the time students complete their AP course, they will have read works from several genres and periods—from the 16th to the 21st century. (College Board AP, 2014, p. 7)

An experienced AP English literature and composition teacher would be able to craft a priority standard to capture the required skill represented in this and other information in the course guide as follows.

> The student is able to analyze, interpret, and evaluate texts in a variety of genres, in a variety of literary periods, 16th to the 21st century.

Obviously, this is an enormous learning target, and it will operate across the entirety of the year of instruction in AP English literature and composition. It is likely that the AP teacher will wish to break this large goal into separate learning targets that he or she addresses sequentially throughout the units of study. But this example proves that it is possible to craft specific priority standards from AP course materials that are useful in focusing curriculum, instruction, assessment, and feedback in the same manner as described in this book with regard to regular K–12 academic standards.

AP test answers are scored on a nine-point scoring rubric. The discrepancy between this rubric and the four-point standards-based learning proficiency scale often challenges AP teachers. As AP students work on their written responses in preparation for the AP test, they should be provided with the nine-point AP score so they can connect the feedback they are being given with projected performance on the national AP test. At the same time, AP teachers will want to record student performance in the grading system on a four-point scale, as with all other work. It is here that using half-point divisions on the four-point scale and using a conversion chart can be very helpful. Thus, teachers can convert the nine-point AP scores into four-point scores as follows (table 5.1).

Table 5.1: Conversion Table for AP Scores

AP Score	Four-Point Score
9	4.0
8	3.5
7	3.0
6	2.5
5	2.0
4	1.5
3	1.0
2	1.0
1	0.5
0	0.0

Teachers can make some adjustments to these equivalencies per their preference, but this chart preserves the College Board informal division of considering as "passing" a score of 5 or above. For instance, teachers may adjust content within a proficiency scale to connect to an AP rubric. In some cases the proficiency scale is more specific and may be used instead of or in addition to the AP rubrics for a particular course. We should note that there is a discrepancy in meaning between the two sides of this chart. For example, if you assign an AP score of 5 (which the College Board might consider passing) to a proficiency scale score of 2.0 (which does not indicate proficiency), it might suggest that the student should not be thought of as passing. This discrepancy is inherent in the different purposes of the two scoring systems. An AP score of 5 is only informally considered passing, and students, in order to achieve a score of 3 (out of 5) on the overall AP test (with the addition of scores from the multiple-choice section of the test) will need to score higher than a 5 on the free-response questions. Converting the nine-point AP scale to the four-point standards-based learning scale allows teachers to roughly equate student progress toward the overall goal of strong performance on the AP test, but there is not a one-to-one equivalency between the two scoring systems, since they are designed to measure different standards of performance.

While the scores on each side of the chart really connect to two different indications of student performance, such that scores on the standards-based learning chart below 2.0 would mean a teacher must provide some help to the student to achieve proficiency, the scores at 2.0 and above more realistically reflect student abilities in the indicated AP skill measured by the nine-point scale.

Standards-Based Learning and International Baccalaureate Classes

Over four thousand schools in North America offer students the opportunity for IB coursework (International Baccalaureate Organization, 2013). The IB offers opportunities for students ages three through nineteen in four programmes (note the European spelling). These include Primary Years (ages three to twelve), Middle Years (ages eleven to sixteen), Diploma (ages sixteen to nineteen), and Career-related (ages sixteen to nineteen). The IB goal is to teach students critical thinking, inquiry, logic, and multilinguistics to prepare them for participating in a global community. As the International Baccalaureate Organization states, "The aim of all IB programmes is to develop internationally minded people who, recognizing their common humanity and shared guardianship of the planet, help to create a better and more peaceful world" (2015, p. 1). IB-trained teachers train students, and these teachers instruct students to take responsibility for their learning by way of a theory of knowledge course. IB students demonstrate their knowledge through consolidations of learning, culminating with the Primary Years' exhibition, the Middle Years' personal project, the Diploma Programme's (DP) extended essay, and the Career-related reflective project. The entire school community may sometimes be involved in providing feedback and support as students demonstrate their knowledge, understanding, and mastery of skills.

IB uses sets of prescribed rubrics and has suggestions for converting such scaled scores into a one-hundred-point scale, as needed. See figure 5.9 for one sample Middle-Years programme (MYP) for tech design.

As you may note, this rubric is similar to a proficiency scale. Yet, you will notice a few distinctions. First, the scale is inverted, noting the highest score at the bottom instead of the top. Next, this is a rubric really designed for assessment. A proficiency scale is broader. Teachers may use it as an assessment tool, and for instruction, goal setting, and tracking progress. We purport that many rubrics inform where a student is on a proficiency scale. Converting the IB rubrics to proficiency scales occurs in a manner similar to the conversion mentioned for AP (see table 5.1, page 115). The IB teacher will break this large goal into separate learning targets that he or she addresses sequentially throughout the units of study. It is possible to craft specific priority standards from IB course materials that are useful in focusing curriculum, instruction, assessment, and feedback in the same manner as described in this book with regard to regular K–12 academic standards.

Gateway High School staff in Aurora, Colorado, merged its work with MYP and DP with the proficiency scales teachers created for the Colorado Academic Standards. The chart in table 5.2 (page 118) displays this alignment. You can see that the MYP and DP rubrics have a scale of 0–8 (shown in the left column), with 8 signifying the highest score and 0 the lowest. The team connected this with the proficiency scale language bolded

Tech Design Assessment Rubric MYP Year One—Grade 6	
Criterion A: Inquiring and Analyzing At the end of year one, the student should be able to: • Explain and justify the need for a solution to a problem • State and prioritize the main points of research he or she needs to develop a solution to the problem • Describe the main features of one existing product that inspires a solution to the problem • Present the main findings of relevant research	
Achievement Level	**Level Descriptor**
0	The student does not reach a standard described by any of the following descriptors.
1–2	The student: • States one basic success criterion for a solution • Presents one design idea, which can be interpreted by others • Creates an incomplete planning drawing or diagram
3–4	The student: • Outlines the need for a solution to a problem • States some points of research he or she needs to develop a solution, with some guidance • States the main features of an existing product that inspires a solution to the problem • Outlines some of the main findings of research
5–6	The student: • Explains the need for a solution to a problem • States and prioritizes the main points of research he or she needs to develop a solution to the problem, with some guidance • Outlines the main features of an existing product that inspires a solution to the problem • Outlines the main findings of relevant research • Develops success criteria for the possible solution
7–8	The student: • Explains and justifies the need for a solution to a problem • States and prioritizes the main points of research he or she needs to develop a solution to the problem, with minimal guidance • Describes the main features of an existing product that inspires a solution to the problem • Presents the main findings of relevant research

Source: Adapted from South Side Middle School, 2017.

Figure 5.9: Sample IB rubric.

and in parentheses following the score. Additionally, the team created a category that also addressed a lack of work submitted, or work that was plagiarized. The center column denotes a corresponding letter grade. This conversion table allows teachers to consider grades across both the applicable IB rubric and the relevant proficiency scale.

Table 5.2: Conversion Table for IB Scores and Letter Grades

Proficiency Grade	Letter Grade	Student Demonstrations
8 **(Advanced)**	A	I demonstrated that I completely understand the concept and requirements by displaying higher-level thinking skills. I demonstrated more complex content.
7 **(Advanced or Proficient+)**	A or B	I demonstrated understanding of the concept by meeting all of the requirements and by beginning some higher-level thinking skills. In addition to level 6 performance, I demonstrated partial success on more complex content.
5–6 **(Proficient)**	B	I demonstrated understanding of the concept by meeting all requirements. I demonstrated the learning target.
3–4 **(Partially Proficient)**	C	I demonstrated a developing or partial understanding of the concept. I demonstrated simpler content.
2 **(Unsatisfactory+)**	D	I demonstrated a minimal understanding of the concept or skill. I demonstrated simpler content with help.
1 (Unsatisfactory)	D or F	Even with support, I demonstrated very minimal understanding of the concept or skill. I demonstrated very minimal content or skill with help.
0 (Unsatisfactory)	F	I did not submit enough work or I submitted work that was not my own. I did not have enough evidence to demonstrate understanding.

Source: © 2017 by Dackri Davis and Gateway High School IB teachers. Used with permission.

Each Gateway High School course uses standards that are taught throughout the year. Teachers evaluate students multiple times on each prioritized standard and give a proficiency score. A student earning an 8 equates to the description of a student fully understanding the concept or skill and displaying higher levels of thinking with this complex content.

A score of 5 or 6 is proficient. This equates in the alignment chart to a grade of B. To earn this 5 or 6 score, a student must demonstrate understanding of the learning target. This is the goal for all students.

A score of 3 or 4 is considered partially proficient. This means that a student could demonstrate a partial understanding of the concept or skill. He or she understands simpler content but has difficulties with complex knowledge and skills. This coincides with a letter grade of C.

Each number on the 0–8 proficiency scale has a grade equivalent and an explanation of the students' demonstrations. When teachers determine a final grade, they look at the assessed prioritized standards, the proficiency scores a student has earned throughout that grading period, and the most-recent proficiency the student demonstrated. Taking all of this into account, teachers can compute a final grade. Teachers use a culmination of quality evidence (mounting evidence) that connects the IB rubrics with the proficiency scales. This evidence supports a more accurate reflection of where students are in their learning and a more accurate final evaluation.

Summary

Standards-based learning environments affect *all* students, yet exceptional situations may need some special considerations. Throughout this chapter, we discussed unique situations and provided guidance for teachers working with students with disabilities, English learners, and gifted students to adapt their proficiency scales and grading methods. We also discussed aligning standards-based grading with students in special classes, including electives, AP, and IB classes. While this chapter provided several conversion options for aligning grading, it is clear that there is no one way to adapt these exceptional situations into a standards-based learning environment.

The following chapter will focus on communicating these figured grades to external stakeholders, including parents and the wider community.

6

Communicating Grades

An oft-used cliché in education states that true change must be staff driven. Strategically communicating with students, parents, colleagues, and the community about the concept of standards-based grading is a critical aspect of teacher leadership. Even if the district or school has a communication plan, individual teachers are often the most effective means of truly getting the message out and accepted. Barnett Berry, Alesha Daughtrey, and Alan Wieder (2010) identified communication as one critical aspect of teacher leadership in school initiatives:

> Prior research has found that a teacher's self-efficacy as an instructional leader is strongly and positively associated with soliciting parent involvement, communicating positive expectations for student learning, improving instructional practice, and being willing (and able) to innovate successfully in the classroom. (p. 1)

Drawing on the critical need to clearly communicate grades to external stakeholders, this chapter will consider several issues key to teacher communication. It will first discuss planning the message to share, including how to effectively communicate *why* standards-based grading practices are different from traditional grading in the most clear and concise manner possible. It will then discuss approaches to parent communication, such as parent-teacher conferences and student-led conferences. Next, the chapter examines how to display standards-based grades on report cards for optimal parent and student understanding of student achievement and progress. Finally, it will address aspects of technology in the standards-based grading process.

The Message

The critical grading message to parents and other external stakeholders should convey two things: (1) the difference between norm-referenced and criterion-referenced grades and how this pertains to standards-based grading, and (2) a common school- or districtwide message, which we will refer to as the *elevator speech*, condensing the explanation of standards-based grading to a consistent set of talking points that will form the basis for all messaging about the concept.

Strategic communication begins with clear planning of this elevator speech. Heflebower et al. (2014) suggested beginning by thinking about three key aspects of communication: "(1) clearly defined goals and desired outcomes; (2) understanding of situational challenges, resources, and allies; and (3) sensitivity toward stakeholder audiences, including allies, skeptics, and vocal dissenters" (p. 93). When developing the speech, teachers should first consider its audience and purpose. Based on the exact audience, teachers may need to customize their message for different target groups to ensure that each group has multiple opportunities to learn and relearn about standards-based grading.

Explaining Norm-Referenced Versus Criterion-Referenced Grades

To communicate effectively about standards-based learning and grading, teachers must first establish the *why* by clarifying the difference between norm-referenced and criterion-referenced education. Traditionally, assessment and grading occurred in a norm-referenced approach, where students were compared with other students. The norm-referenced approach relies heavily on the concept of the traditional bell-curve distribution of student performance. However, the No Child Left Behind Act, which Congress passed in 2001 and then-President George W. Bush signed into law on January 8, 2002, ushered in a new, criterion-referenced era of education in the United States. Similar legislative acts in other countries have had the same effect around the world. This marked the beginning of education's criterion-referenced standards era.

A criterion-referenced approach compares student performance to the criterion or standards that are set forth for students to learn. Grading in a criterion format needs to reflect the progress a student is making toward each standard. Traditional grading practices do not align well with criterion education or provide information that reflects an individual student's progress and learning. Many parents, students, and members of the public thus do not grasp the distinction between these two concepts. Taking time to communicate the differences will help clarify how the approach to education has changed since 2001. Clarifying these differences also begins to establish the need for adjusting grading practices to accurately reflect student progress in a system based on standards.

This message needs to be concise and easy to understand while at the same time drawing clear attention to differences. The information in table 6.1 is from definitions of norm-referenced and criterion-referenced testing found on the website *The Glossary of Educational Reform. The Glossary of Educational Reform* (Great Schools Partnership, 2014) is a nonprofit, online resource established to help inform journalists, parents, and community members about school-improvement strategies and concepts. The comparison of norm-referenced and criterion-referenced grading in the table identifies important points for this message.

Table 6.1: Norm-Referenced Versus Criterion-Referenced Grading

Norm Referenced	Criterion Referenced
This grading: • Compares and ranks a student's performance against other students' performances • Generally, reports scores as a percentile ranking within a group • Is based on bell curve expectations, where some students do well, most are average, and some do poorly	This grading: • Measures an individual student's performance against a set of criteria established as standards • Indicates an individual student's level of proficiency in relation to specific standards • Allows for the possibility that all students may do well if they can demonstrate the knowledge and skills explicit in the standards

Source: Great Schools Partnership, 2014.

Knowing the Elevator Speech

Ideally, the district or school will initiate and organize communication about standards-based grading. However, individual teachers must be able to communicate the concept and field questions about it with a confident level of understanding. An important strategy for this purpose is to develop a common message or *elevator speech* about the concept and process of standard-based grading that teachers may share with colleagues, students, parents, and community members. Heflebower et al. (2014) explained this strategy:

> An elevator speech distills a message down to its most important elements. The following is an example of an elevator speech for standards-based grading:

> As you may know, the role of our staff is to educate all students to proficient levels. In order to do so, we are revising our grading practices to be aligned to the standards students must meet. That way, grades will be a clearer indication of what students have learned, not simply a measure of how much work they can turn in or how hard they might try in class. Learning is the indicator of success. (pp. 94–95)

The talking points for the elevator speech are best created collaboratively so teachers are consistent and accurate in their communication. If this is not done as a district or schoolwide strategy, we highly advise teacher teams or individual teachers to engage in this step of preparation for grading conversations and questions.

Once the elevator speech has been developed, teachers and administrators can embed it within larger messages as they develop information to begin educating parents, students, and other colleagues about the concept of standards-based grading. An example of this can be seen in the following vignette from Northwood, North Dakota, teachers Jaci Lenz and Sarah Burger (personal communication, December 27, 2017). After developing their talking points, they created a presentation to educate students and parents.

When we made the change to standards-based grading, we knew that communicating with parents and students would be essential to the success of our efforts. Before we could create our message, we needed to clarify our beliefs and expectations. We made sure they were the same, which ensured that the students would experience similar things in both classes.

From these beliefs we formed a presentation for parents, which we delivered at our back-to-school event. Parents and students from each grade level met at different times throughout the night. During the presentation, we discussed in depth our reasons for switching from traditional grading systems and what they could expect from the new system. We explained how proficiency scales work, what the scores at each level represent, and how students would track their own progress. In addition, parents were provided with sample scales from both subjects. We gave parents and students a chance to ask questions. Each family received a standards-based grading handbook, which communicated these same ideas.

It was important to us that the communication didn't stop at this meeting, so we sent home newsletters to the parents, which reminded them about what they would see in the gradebook and what their children were learning. We met with parents again at parent-teacher conferences. At report card time, we attached reports that showed not only the summative score, but all the formative scores as well. This allowed the parents to see the growth their child experienced over the year.

Parent Communication

Parents constitute one of the most important and critical audiences to communicate with when it comes to grades. For many parents, the concept of standards-based grading is completely different from their traditional paradigm of grading. One simple question sums up the core of their interest: How will this affect my child? Answering that question should provide guidance to teachers when communicating with parents.

One of the most effective methods of communicating about grading with parents is ensuring students clearly understand the concepts and processes of standards-based learning and grading. Students who clearly understand proficiency scales and how they relate to grades can often help educate their parents. One strategy is to have students create their own proficiency scales that demonstrate the progressions of learning for a self-selected aspect of their life. This gives students a personal connection and understanding about what a proficiency scale is and how it relates to their own development of a process or skill. Students can use the scale they create to communicate the concept of proficiency scales to their parents without having academic content involved (see figure 6.1). A student who enjoys basketball might develop this scale as he or she is learning about the concept of proficiency scales and their relationship to learning and grades.

4.0 Advanced	I can dribble a basketball between my legs and behind my back while running up the court.
3.0 Proficient	I can dribble a basketball with either hand while running up the court.
	I can dribble a basketball back and forth between hands while running up the court.
2.0 Progressing	I can dribble a basketball with my right hand while walking.
	I can dribble a basketball with my left hand while walking.
	I can dribble back and forth between my right and left hands while walking.

Figure 6.1: Student self-created proficiency scale example.

In addition to student-parent communication, explicit communication from teacher to parent about the standards-based-grading process will also be necessary. This communication can occur in a variety of ways, and teachers should make an informed choice about the method of communication they'll use for this purpose based on their individual situations. The use of social media might be one vehicle a teacher can use. A Pew Research Center study found that 79 percent of adults identified Facebook as their most-used online platform while 24 percent identified Twitter (Greenwood, Perrin, & Duggan, 2016). These social media tools can provide an efficient vehicle to deliver short, informative chunks of information to parents both *en masse* and individually regarding their own child's learning. Quick pictures of students tracking their own progress or short videos of students discussing their level of understanding based on a proficiency scale can help solidify the concept of student learning and how the standards-based grading process reflects it.

As part of the communication process, teachers can also provide clear descriptions for students and parents to use as they view student scores. Figure 6.2 provides an example of a scale-score translation that can help communicate the meaning of scores as they relate to student knowledge and progress.

Scores and Descriptors	Progressions of Learning
4.0 Advanced	Evidence clearly demonstrates knowledge and skills above the level the standards identified.
3.5	Evidence indicates growth in student knowledge and skills beyond proficiency in the standards.

Figure 6.2: Scale-score translation guide for students and parents.

Continued →

Scores and Descriptors	Progressions of Learning
3.0 Proficient	Evidence clearly demonstrates knowledge and skill that meets the standards.
2.5	Evidence indicates knowledge and skills beyond the foundations and moving toward proficiency in the standards.
2.0 Progressing	Evidence indicates knowledge and skills of the foundational concepts for the standards.
1.5	Evidence indicates growth in student knowledge and skills beyond beginning levels of understanding.
1.0 Beginning	Evidence indicates beginning stages of knowledge and skills with assistance from the teacher.

This section will discuss two avenues of teacher-to-parent communication: (1) parent-teacher conferences and (2) student-led conferences.

Parent-Teacher Conferences

Parent-teacher conferences offer one of the most powerful opportunities for communication about learning and grading. Using proficiency scales as the basis for conversation in parent-teacher conferences provides several advantages that can enrich the conversation and engage parents in a productive discussion about standards-based learning and grading.

First, using scales offers parents an accurate view of the standards the state (or province) has set forth for their child to learn. For many parents this will be the first time they actively take a look at the standards and have an opportunity to understand what their child is learning. Teachers can explain the specific standards by showing parents level 3.0 of the scale and helping them to understand what that specific standard is asking their child to do in order to meet the standard. Second, teachers can use level 2.0 to help parents understand the prerequisite skills that are necessary for students to possess in order to achieve proficiency. Often, these are the skills that can provide parents with specific ideas about how to help their children at home. One common question parents ask is, What can we do to help him or her at home? Level 2.0 of the scale can provide parents with specific vocabulary or foundational learning to answer that question. Third, level 4.0 of the scale provides specific information about differentiating the curriculum for students who are in need of extensions or higher levels of cognitive challenge in their learning.

The use of scales in conferences also allows a teacher to connect the concepts of scale scores and summative scores to student knowledge gain over time. Teachers can also show artifacts of student work or assessments that correlate to the levels of the proficiency scale in order to help parents see how student scores relate directly to their assessment scores. In cases where a student may not yet be proficient, parents can see he or she is still working and will have future opportunities to demonstrate growth.

It has been our common experience to hear teachers who use proficiency scales as the basis for parent-teacher conferences say these conferences are more productive and more focused on learning, and that they help parents understand the concept of standards-based learning and grading.

Student-Led Conferences

As more and more schools move from parent-teacher to student-led conferences, proficiency scales can play an increasingly critical supporting role. The purpose of a student-led conference is to allow the student to take the lead and explain to his or her parents what he or she is learning and how the student sees his or her personal progression in that learning.

Using the scales as the basis for conversations helps students communicate their current level of proficiency on the scale, what they are doing well, and where they need to grow. When appropriate, having students share examples of how they are tracking their own progress helps parents see how students can own their own learning and understand where they are in their current progression of learning.

For student-led conferences, each teacher should have scales available for the priority standards that he or she assesses during the reporting period. Teachers may also want to include scales that represent knowledge that they will monitor for student growth across multiple reporting periods. During the conference, students can use the proficiency scales in conjunction with their standards-referenced report cards to explain their current level of proficiency in each of the standards. In this format, students can show examples of their work and communicate which level of the scale their work currently represents for specific standards.

One strategy that works well is for teachers to work with students to select a specific scale (or two) that demonstrates how their learning increased in a specific topic (or two) as they display artifacts of their work. Teachers can use a script for students to follow as they discuss their learning. A typical script for this purpose follows five steps.

1. Introduce the topic and explain the different levels on the scale.

2. Explain which level you were on the scale at the beginning of the topic.

3. Explain one or two important ideas you learned about the topic.

4. Explain your growth on the levels of the scale and where you are now.

5. Talk about how you feel personally about your learning and growth.

Report Cards

The most prevalent form of communication of student progress is the report card. Done well, a report card can communicate a valid representation of student progress. Heflebower et al. (2014) identify key aspects for report cards:

> The following three elements should be included on any report card. First, a report card should explain the priority standards that are important for each grade level or content area. Second, a report card should explain the proficiency-scale-based method to assign grades. . . . Third, a report card should report students' scores for the prioritized standards and their scores for life skills (such as work habits, attendance and so on) separately. (p. 66)

In a standards-based learning environment, it makes the most sense to use a standards-based or standards-referenced report card. *Standards-referenced reporting* (Marzano, 2010) is the process of reporting a student's status on each priority standard based on the proficiency scale levels. Standards-referenced reporting occurs by figuring a summative score for each priority standard that is taught during a reporting period. In standards-referenced reporting a student may or may not be proficient in all the priority standards when they progress to the next grade level or course.

Figure 6.3 shows a section of a standards-referenced report card. It reports a student's academic scores for each topic (proficiency scale) covered in class during the grading period: three standards for reading, five standards for writing, and four standards for speaking and listening. It also reports individual scores for the nonacademic skills of participation, work completion, behavior, and working in groups. The light-colored bars on each row of the report card indicates a student's final status for a particular measurement topic. The dark bars represent a student's initial status for each measurement topic. This system allows students and parents to see growth in addition to final scores.

Language Arts		0.0	0.5	1.0	1.5	2.0	2.5	3.0	3.5	4.0
Reading										
Word Recognition and Vocabulary	3.5									
Reading for Main Idea	2.5									
Literary Analysis	3.0									
Writing										
Language Conventions	4.0									
Organization and Focus	2.0									
Research and Technology	1.5									
Evaluation and Revision	2.5									
Writing Applications	1.0									

Speaking and Listening		
Comprehension	3.0	
Organization and Delivery	3.5	
Analysis and Evaluation of Media	2.0	
Speaking Applications	2.0	
Work Habits		
Participation	4.0	
Work Completion	3.0	
Behavior	4.0	
Working in Groups	2.5	

Sources: *Adapted from Marzano, 2010, pp. 115–117.*

Figure 6.3 Standards-referenced report card for ELA and life skills.

The complete report card would have a similar section for each course or content area.

We will now discuss in greater detail the issues relating to converting scores to letter or percentage grades and communicating nonacademic factors such as work habits and effort.

Converting to Letter or Percentage Grades

Because parents and other stakeholders may not completely understand standards-based or standards-referenced grades, some schools elect to convert proficiency scale scores to traditional omnibus grades such as letter or percentage grades. Once teachers figure summative grades for different topics or standards in a reporting period, two additional steps can help teachers convert standards-referenced grades to course or subject grades in a traditional format. The first step is to average the different summative grades that have been assigned for each different standard or topic during the reporting period. Averaging the summative grades is perfectly acceptable because each summative grade represents a different topic or standard and because this average does not "steal" learning from students since it occurs using their final status on different topics. The second step is to use a conversion table that shows where the average of the summative grades would fall in the school's traditional grading system. It is important to note the use of conversion tables is a school-based decision, and all teachers should consistently use one conversion table to report in a traditional format. Table 6.2 (page 130) shows an example of a conversion scale from standards-referenced grades measured in 0.5 increments to traditional letter grades. Table 6.2 uses and suggests pluses and minuses. This assists in showing growth for students, especially struggling learners, even when using traditional grading methods.

Table 6.2: Conversion Table for Letter Grades

A+	3.75–4.00	B+	2.84–2.99	C+	2.34–2.49	D+	1.76–1.99
A	3.26–3.74	B	2.67–2.83	C	2.17–2.33	D	1.26–1.75
A-	3.00–3.25	B–	2.50–2.66	C-	2.00–2.16	D–	1.00–1.25
						F	Below 1.00

Source: Marzano, 2010, p. 106.

Table 6.3 shows both steps of this process using a sample conversion table to the complete one-hundred-point scale. This sample conversion scale first indicates how teachers can convert each point on the one-hundred-point scale to the proficiency scale score. Second, it shows how many opportunities there are for students to fail (the white sections on the scale). The picture denotes this quite dramatically. It is important to reiterate that the school or district should approve and adopt any conversion scale it uses, and the school or district should consistently apply it. In other words, it would be futile for the social sciences department to use a different conversion scale to that of the art department. The rationale is simple: consistency among teachers, through using a similar scale, assists in providing more reliable interpretations of student performance.

Communicating Nonacademic Factors

One of the key communication aspects in standards-based grading is the purposeful separation of academic knowledge and student behavior. Traditional grading approaches blend factors such as work completion and participation into a single subject or course grade. In fact, traditional grading systems camouflage these factors and can provide misleading information. For example, if a student receives a traditional grade of 86 percent, it appears at face value that the student is in the low B range and has a fair but not strong grasp of the content. However, the truth for this student could be that he or she knows the content extremely well but has had points deducted from his or her grade for continually turning in late work. The academic work he or she does is accurate and deserving of a higher mark. However, a traditional system for reporting grades doesn't separate these two factors in order to get to the root cause of the matter.

As we discussed earlier in this chapter (see Report Cards, page 128), proficiency scales for behavior or life skills should be in place. Using proficiency scales clarifies expectations for behaviors and work habits to provide parents and students with a clear picture of these factors as part of the learning and development process. Using separate scales for nonacademic factors can help teachers better affect student behavior through a learning approach rather than just a discipline approach. Nonacademic proficiency scales also allow teachers to clearly communicate a student's progress or lack of progress in very specific and important aspects, such as work completion and effort, on the report card.

Table 6.3: Conversion Table for One Hundred–Point Scale

Average Scale Score	Percentage	Grade	Average Scale Score	Percentage	Grade	Average Scale Score	Percentage	Grade	Average Scale Score	Percentage	Grade
4.00	100	A	1.86–1.99	76	D	0.80	50	F	0.49–0.50	25	F
3.86–3.99	99	A	1.72–1.85	75	D	0.79	49	F	0.47–0.48	24	F
3.72–3.85	98	A	1.58–1.71	74	D	0.78	48	F	0.45–0.46	23	F
3.58–3.71	97	A	1.44–1.57	73	D	0.77	47	F	0.43–0.44	22	F
3.44–3.57	96	A	1.30–1.43	72	D	0.76	46	F	0.41–0.42	21	F
3.30–3.43	95	A	1.15–1.29	71	D	0.75	45	F	0.39–0.40	20	F
3.15–3.29	94	A	1.00–1.14	70	D	0.74	44	F	0.37–0.38	19	F
3.00–3.14	93	A	0.99	69	F	0.73	43	F	0.35–0.36	18	F
	92	B	0.98	68	F	0.72	42	F	0.33–0.34	17	F
	91	B	0.97	67	F	0.71	41	F	0.31–0.32	16	F
	90	B	0.96	66	F	0.70	40	F	0.29–0.30	15	F
	89	B	0.95	65	F	0.69	39	F	0.27–0.28	14	F
	88	B	0.94	64	F	0.68	38	F	0.25–0.26	13	F
	87	B	0.93	63	F	0.67	37	F	0.23–0.24	12	F
	86	B	0.92	62	F	0.66	36	F	0.21–0.22	11	F
	85	B	0.91	61	F	0.65	35	F	0.19–0.20	10	F
	84	C	0.90	60	F	0.64	34	F	0.17–0.18	9	F
	83	C	0.89	59	F	0.63	33	F	0.15–0.16	8	F
	82	C	0.88	58	F	0.62	32	F	0.13–0.14	7	F
	81	C	0.87	57	F	0.61	31	F	0.11–0.12	6	F
	80	C	0.86	56	F	0.59–0.60	30	F	0.09–0.10	5	F
	79	C	0.85	55	F	0.57–0.58	29	F	0.07–0.08	4	F
	78	C	0.84	54	F	0.55–0.56	28	F	0.05–0.06	3	F
	77	C	0.83	53	F	0.53–0.54	27	F	0.03–0.04	2	F
			0.82	52	F	0.51–0.52	26	F	0.01–0.02	1	F
			0.81	51	F				0.00	0	F

Source: Marzano, 2018.

Figure 6.4 shows a general report card example. This format reports the student's summative scores and converted traditional scores for language arts, mathematics, science, social studies, and art on the left. On the right, are summative work habit scores for participation, work completion, behavior, and working in groups.

Language Arts	C (2.46)	Participation	A (3.40)
Mathematics	B (2.50)	Work Completion	B (2.90)
Science	C (2.20)	Behavior	A (3.40)
Social Studies	A (3.10)	Working in Groups	B (2.70)
Art	A (3.00)		

Source: Heflebower et al., 2014, p. 68.

Figure 6.4: General report card.

The report card section in figure 6.5 illustrates a different way to report academic and nonacademic grades. Prioritized standards or key assignments are on the left with the student's academic scores for each item, while the student's work habit grade for timeliness is on the right.

Social Studies			
Learning Target or Assignment		Life Skill (Timeliness)	
11.2.4 Civil War Battle Map	3.0	Late one day	2.0
11.5.6 Cause and Effect of War	2.5	On time	3.0

Source: Heflebower et al., 2014, p. 68.

Figure 6.5: Report card with academic grades and work habits.

A key aspect of standards-based grading is the opportunity to implement productive changes, additions, and clarifications to how teachers report grades. Report cards can clearly show a student's level of proficiency for specific standards as well as the student's current status on academic or behavior skills. By using a conversion table, a school can also have the option of converting standards-based grades to a traditional format if they need to do so.

In reporting student progress, technology and apps are available to help teachers and schools accomplish grade communication in an effective manner. The next section will address key aspects of using technology for the purpose of communicating grades.

Technology and Grade Communication

A common hurdle in the communication of standards-based grading is the use of current technologies and student-management systems. The majority of these systems have been set up to figure a basic average for students in a traditional one hundred–point scale. This can be a frustrating hurdle for teachers, and in some cases, it becomes the roadblock that inhibits the move to standards-based grading. There are, however, new players in this arena, and some student-management systems are beginning to offer versions of their software that are more compatible with a standards-based approach. However, there are ways to use traditional systems in a more standards-based manner. One simple change is to set up gradebook categories based on priority standards or topics that will be taught rather than types of tasks. Instead of categories such as tests, quizzes, and homework, the gradebook categories become the specific standards that are being taught during a reporting period. A teacher will still use tests, quizzes, and homework, but the results of each will be collected to show student progress within a specific topic or standard. Heflebower et al. (2014) provided an example of this approach:

> The following story explains how a teacher modified her grading practices by adjusting her gradebook. Kristin Poage changed her gradebook headings from labels like Homework, Classwork, Tests, and Quizzes to standards-based headings such as 7.3.2 Writing Revision and 10.4.3 Reading Comprehension. First, this forced her to only give assignments and grades based on standards. Second, it made it easy for her to identify and target struggling students with interventions. With the previous headings, if a student failed to meet the target score in the area of Homework, Kristin had no information about what interventions would be most effective for that student. However, failure to meet the target for 7.3.2 Writing Revision gave Kristin a clearer indication of what remediation and intervention was needed. (p. 69)

An additional aspect of communication through technology involves students and parents viewing grades as they post. This is a viable option and will provide an opportunity to again communicate with and train parents on how to view standards-based grading. This will fall naturally into the communication flow about the grading process, and there are different ways to approach this. One way is to engage students in viewing grades with their parents and explaining what the different scores indicate and how they relate to the student's progress in learning. If grades are entered as proficiency level scores for a specific standard or topic, students can show their parents the progression of scores and explain the meaning in relationship to their current knowledge. If teachers provide parents with a scale-score translation guide, such as the one figure 6.2 (page 125) shows, they can look at scores entered into an electronic gradebook and see an articulated pattern of learning for their child. Consider the following example of a gradebook set up for standards-based learning (figure 6.6). A parent using the translation guide in figure 6.2 can see his or her child's growth in knowledge and also recognize the meaning of each specific score.

Standard	Score	Score	Score	Score	Score	Score
7.1 Main Idea	2.0	2.5	3.0	3.0		
7.2 Literature Analysis	2.0	2.0	3.0			

Figure 6.6: Gradebook example of student scores.

Summary

Teachers can be the single most effective communicators for the transition to standards-based grading. Helping parents understand the difference between norm-referenced and criterion-referenced education is a key starting point. Teachers should collaboratively craft a core message about standards-based grading that identifies key concepts that will consistently appear in communication with colleagues, students, parents, and the community as a whole.

Parent-teacher conferences, including student-led conferences, provide additional opportunities to communicate the concept and demonstrate how it relates directly to standards-based learning. The use of proficiency scales in these conferences helps keep the focus clearly on learning. Likewise, the use of proficiency scales for separating academic and nonacademic skills provides an additional window into the learning process that is often hidden in traditional grading and reporting.

As with any new concept, communication about the standards-based grading process needs to be ongoing. Ensuring that students understand the process will prepare them to assist their parents in understanding. Using various media and providing aids that help parents learn and relearn the concept of standards-based grading helps build a consistent and informed message.

Epilogue

Transitioning to standards-based learning is a process. In order for this work to be solidified, collaborative cultures and productive structures are necessary. As Heflebower et al. (2014) stated, "Teachers need time to process with one another, try new ideas, receive feedback from peers, and—over time—change existing philosophies. A culture of support, trust, and modeling is important" (p. 113).

This work coincides well with the educational initiatives many districts have in progress. Standards-based learning is a particularly significant topic for schools who are interested in becoming high reliability organizations. High reliability organizations are those that "take a variety of extraordinary steps in pursuit of error-free performance" (Weick, Sutcliffe, & Obstfeld, 1999, p. 33). Robert J. Marzano, Philip B. Warrick, Cameron L. Rains, and Richard DuFour (2019) suggested that schools could become high reliability organizations and detailed five levels that schools need to work on to make the transition to becoming a High Reliability School (HRS), as shown in table E.1.

Table E.1: Levels of Operation for a High Reliability School

Level 5	Competency-based education
Level 4	Standards-referenced reporting
Level 3	Guaranteed and viable curriculum
Level 2	Effective teaching in every classroom
Level 1	Safe, supportive, and collaborative culture

Source: Adapted from Marzano et al., 2019, pp. 31–32.

Levels 3, 4, and 5 of the model specifically address standards-based learning. The practices, strategies, and guidelines in this book are foundational to making the shifts required by those levels. Chapters 1, 2, and 3 directly connect to the notion of HRS level 2 (*effective teaching in every classroom*). In fact, these chapters assist teachers with any framework for instruction, as they help teachers with the planning, instruction, goal setting, and progress tracking required in any learning environment. Chapter 4 specifically connects to the *guaranteed and viable curriculum* of level 3; it outlines the strategies helpful in making this HRS level come to life in a practical manner through administering quality classroom assessments. It also connects to HRS level 4 (*standards-referenced reporting*) by assisting teachers through the tedious, yet critical, process of figuring grades. Chapters 5 and 6 work in concert to provide support to teachers of exceptional students as well as connecting the figuring to the effective communicating of grades. All of these chapters are foundational toward guiding teachers to the competency-based system that is the focus of HRS level 5, where students matriculate based on their knowledge of the content, rather than time spent in class.

Just as there are High Reliability Schools, there are also High Reliability Teachers™ (HRT; for more information, see www.MarzanoResources.com/hrs/hrt). This book also supports the levels described for HRTs. In fact, levels 1, 3, and 4 of HRT (*foundation of instructional strategies*, *student learning*, and *valid and rigorous feedback*) provide support for those interested in focusing efforts on the continuous improvement process.

This resource is also complementary to successful implementation of *The New Art and Science of Teaching* (Marzano, 2017). All of the chapters in *A Teacher's Guide to Standards-Based Learning* address the major category of feedback, although this resource goes into particular depth and detail for two elements of this category: (1) providing and communicating clear learning goals and (2) using assessments (Marzano, 2017). *A Teacher's Guide to Standards-Based Learning* is not only useful in deeper implementation of this instructional framework; it can also be applied to other frameworks.

Teachers and leaders who commit to standards-based learning propel their schools to the highest levels of reliability and effectiveness. Addressing the issue of standards-based learning not only moves schools into a more highly reliable system but also tackles some of the most concerning inconsistencies in our existing systems.

Appendix A:
Frequently Asked Questions

Over many years of leading workshops for administrators and teachers facing the shift to standards-based learning, we have found that many of the same questions emerge. In this section, we have captured several of those frequently asked questions, and we offer some quick answers as well as guidance about where to find additional information on each subject within the body of the book.

Procedure and Policy

How do teachers handle new students arriving in the middle of the year, semester, or unit, who may not have sufficient background in the particular unit or standard under instruction?

Regardless of the system of instruction and assessment—whether traditional or standards based—the situation of accommodating a new student's needs to the class is difficult. In a standards-based environment, an essential first step is a benchmark assessment based on the scales being taught at the time of the student's arrival. From the data of that assessment, create a *merger plan*, which addresses the student's needs and identifies areas in which he or she must quickly catch up with the class to best allow him or her to assimilate to the learning progression of the class as a whole. The timeframe should be as quick as possible, but also realistic in terms of the gains the new student must make.

For a short period of time, it will be necessary to differentiate instruction. This can be more than different in-class activities. Consider the possibilities of online instruction or reteaching modules that can allow the student to make progress quickly. When assigning grades for the merger period, base them on the evidence the student provides about prior learning and the growth the student makes on the current proficiency scale. For more detailed information, refer to the section on Figuring Grades (page 82).

Why shouldn't a teacher count homework as a grade but still use it as a practice?

Teachers can count homework for a grade, although they should consider it student practice of knowledge and skill and part of the learning progression. The larger issue with regard to counting homework in the gradebook concerns authorship. Work done outside of class is work done away from the teacher's control, and in the end, there is no guarantee that the student did his or her own work. As teachers report scores in the gradebook by standard, the purpose of recording those scores is to assemble a body of evidence for student performance to a standard. Work that may not be the student's own could mean that the body of evidence does not accurately represent the student's performance.

Priority Standards and Proficiency Scales

What makes a good proficiency scale?

A high-quality proficiency scale aligns to one or more learning targets of a priority standard and hits the *sweet spot* between being too broad and too narrow. See chapter 1 (page 7) for details on making judgments about how comprehensive a scale should be, as well as for recommendations about specificity, clarity, and the structural elements of scales. Because a proficiency scale is essential to standards-based learning, it needs to be as accurate as possible, defining the sufficient detail of what a student should know and be able to do at each level. At the same time, proficiency scales are not documents carved in stone. As with any important element of instruction and assessment, proficiency scales should be subject to review and adjustment. Teachers just starting to use proficiency scales should not be afraid to take their best shot and be ready to adjust. While the proficiency scale is key, the expectation should not be perfection. Teachers and students are resilient, and they can adjust to minor changes in the proficiency scale during the school year.

What is the difference between a rubric and a proficiency scale?

Rubrics and proficiency scales share many common features, but they are substantially different. Educators use both for offering feedback to students, and both have scores associated with levels of performance. Rubrics are usually for a specific product, project, or task. Proficiency scales, on the other hand, are for a broader conceptual understanding represented by the priority standard or particular learning target. (For more details on the concept of proficiency scales, see Marzano, 2010.) Proficiency scales provide a framework for instruction on a priority standard or learning target and a framework for assessment on that goal or target. For more information, see chapter 1 ("Planning Instruction With Proficiency Scales," page 7), chapter 2 ("Instructing With Proficiency Scales," page 35), and chapter 4 ("Administering Quality Classroom Assessments and Figuring Grades," page 71).

How do I handle multiple and sequential standards in a single unit?

Nearly every teacher will face this challenge, since in most content areas the standards are not purely sequential in the sense that only one is the focus at a time. Some content areas are primarily sequential, such as mathematics and science, and some are rarely sequential, such as English language arts. In managing multiple standards, it is important to carefully plan the unit of instruction with related standards, ones that logically are taught together. For more information, see chapter 2 ("Instructing With Proficiency Scales," page 35). Experienced teachers who have developed student knowledge and skills over the years will be able to make good judgments about the relationship of standards to each other and how they can be logically grouped.

Assessment can follow the instructional plan by grouping multiple standards in a single assessment. In this case, the student would receive more than one score for the assessment, since the teacher provides a separate score for each assessed priority standard. The teacher would record these scores in separate locations in the gradebook by standard. If students are tracking personal goals on priority standards, it is important that the teacher separates the scores and clearly associates each score to a standard so that students can record the information on their goal-tracking forms. Keep in mind that students can track more than one standard at a time, but that their focus will dissipate if we ask them to track many at a time. A good rule of thumb is two or three at the elementary level, but no more than five at the secondary level. For more information, see chapter 3 ("Setting Goals and Tracking Progress," page 47) and chapter 4 ("Administering Quality Classroom Assessments and Figuring Grades," page 71).

How could teachers apply standards-based learning to subjects such as social studies, art, physical education, and so on?

If the state (or province) or the school district provides a set of standards for the content area, these standards should be the starting point for identifying priority standards and creating proficiency scales as chapter 1 (page 7) indicated. In following this process, teachers should also consider college-and-work-readiness standards from the state (or province) or school district, as these standards apply to all classes. Teachers should keep in mind the shift toward standards representing what students should know and be able to do, as opposed to experiencing a sequence of content. As stated in chapter 2 ("Instructing With Proficiency Scales," page 35), the content should serve the standards.

The process of identifying priority standards and creating proficiency scales is more challenging when there are no state (or province) or school district standards available. This can sometimes be the case with elective classes such as music, art, business, and so forth. The process is even more challenging when a teacher takes on the identification of priority standards and creating scales as the *only teacher* instructing the class at the school or in the school district. In this case, the teacher is on his or her own and does not have access to colleagues' expertise. National standards that organizations of teachers create by content area are sometimes a good starting place for teachers in this situation. A Google search will also often find school districts that have made the transition to standards-based learning and offer their priority standards and proficiency scales online. While we do not recommend any teacher simply "lift" premade standards and scales for his or her class, seeing what other educators in the field have done can be helpful in guiding teachers in their own decision making.

Assessment

How many assessments do teachers need per quarter, semester, or year?

The number of assessments teachers require will depend on many factors, including the complexity of the standard and its associated learning targets and students' background knowledge. Therefore, there is no set number of assessments that we can recommend. Rather, teachers must use their own judgment on this issue. The purpose of assessing student performance is to create a body of evidence that supports the decisions the teacher will make when assigning current performance scores (during the learning period) or the summative score (at the end of the learning period). The key question to keep in mind when assigning these scores is, Can I make an accurate inference about this student's performance on this priority standard? Sufficient evidence will help make the answer to this question a "*yes!*" In judging whether the evidence is sufficient, teachers should be careful to not allow a single score to carry too much weight, as teachers can never make an important judgment about student performance based on a single data point (see page 85). If the answer to the question about making an accurate inference about student performance on a standard is *no*, it likely indicates that additional assessments are necessary. For more detailed discussion, see chapter 4 ("Administering Quality Classroom Assessments and Figuring Grades," page 71).

Grading in a Standards-Based Classroom

How do teachers grade students who are frequently absent if zeros are not recommended? Why do students who turn in late work still receive full credit?

Considering the role of a zero in grading is where the answer to these questions is found. If, as the proficiency scale indicates, a zero means that "Even with help, the student has no success," then using a zero reports that no learning on a priority standard is evidenced. If, on the other hand, the teacher uses a zero to measure student compliance with teacher expectations, the zero is a measure of student behavior, not academic performance on a priority standard. A student who turns in late work may not be meeting the teacher's expectations with regard to getting work in on time, but that student may very well be turning in high-quality work *with regard to the priority standard the assignment is measuring*. In this case, the student would receive a strong grade for work on the priority standard; the teacher may elect to also grade the student on a separate standard related to getting work in on time, and the student would receive a score below standard on that scale, possibly even a zero.

The question of grading students who are frequently absent is somewhat more complicated than previously indicated. The purpose of assessment is to judge a student's progress on each priority standard the teacher is assessing during the learning period. To do this, the teacher should create a body of evidence to support the judgment of the student's progress on each standard. The teacher reports that judgment as the student's current score on each standard. If the student is often absent, it becomes very difficult for the teacher to assemble that body of evidence. If the student's absence is justified, such as for an extended medical problem, the teacher will work with the parents and student during and after the absence to provide work and guide the student's growth when he or she returns.

More often, though, students are chronically absent without justification. In this case, the first step is to address the absences through the existing administrative means available. When the student returns, the teacher still needs to assemble a body of evidence for each assessed priority standard. This likely means make-up work, but teachers should consider whether every assessment that all other students have completed is necessary to assemble such a body of evidence. A student may be able to show proficiency on some standards after just three or four assignments or assessments. In this case, there is little need for the additional make-up work (just as there would be little need for additional assessments for a student who has been in class and thoroughly demonstrated proficiency). Standards-based learning provides some flexibility to educators in situations where students miss a substantial number of school days and need reintegration into class. For more information, please see chapter 4 ("Administering Quality Assessments and Figuring Grades," page 71).

Although teachers should discourage the use of zeros, is there ever a time where a zero is justified?

In referring to the generic descriptions of levels in a proficiency scale, a zero means that "Even with help, the student has no success" (Marzano, 2010). If this is what we mean when we assign a zero to a student's performance, this question is really asking, "Is there ever a situation in which a student does not demonstrate success?"

Every student can learn, but this does not mean that every student can learn at the same level of performance. Even with a menu of interventions that the teacher accesses at appropriate moments in the learning period to support the learning a student can do, there may be some students who cannot demonstrate performance above the 0.0 level on the proficiency scale, and assigning a score of 0.0 is appropriate in this situation. Note that this assumes that the teacher intervened on multiple occasions throughout the learning period and made every attempt to improve student performance. For more information on zeros, refer to page 88 or see Marzano, 2010.

How do teachers determine proficiency for students who refuse to do work or complete assessments?

While it is true that involving students in their own learning by sharing standards and proficiency scales with them and allowing them to set and track their own learning through the methods described in chapters 2 and 3 will change the attitude of many students about school, there are often students who remain disconnected from the activities done in class. Teachers who find this to be the case have a couple of options.

If it is necessary to include students' behavior (in the form of assessing completion and timeliness of work) in the students' overall grade, the important issue is to avoid combining behavior with academic performance. Teachers can create a separate set of standards and proficiency scales that address these important life skills (see page 90). In this case, we recommend that behavior count for no more than ten percent of the students' overall, or omnibus, grade in the class.

If the problem remains broader than a few recalcitrant students, teachers may be dealing with a larger cultural issue in the school or its community. At this point there are limits to what individual teachers can do beyond inspiring good behavior, and the issue should be dealt with at the administrative level with a schoolwide effort to affect student behavior.

For classes like physical education, where wearing the gym uniform each class counts as a majority percentage of a student's grade, how would grading change when standards-based grading is fully implemented?

This issue addresses the separation between academic performance and behavior. A look at typical physical education standards will reveal that from an academic standpoint, physical education teachers are to teach and assess performance in areas such as physical fitness, physical and emotional wellness, and risk management in physical education. These areas, as with most academic standards, do not specifically address student behavior in class. Thus, if teachers are to measure student knowledge and ability growth on the academic standards in physical education, they would not be reporting performance on issues such as dressing properly for class.

Teachers who feel that it is important to develop responsible students by making behavior a part of their overall grade can create separate standards and proficiency scales for issues such as being properly ready to learn in class. When this is done, we strongly recommend that this portion account for no more than ten percent of the students' overall, or omnibus, score in the class. For more detailed information, refer to page 90.

How will standards-based grading affect college admissions?

A standards-based report card usually reports student performance by standard. In our experience of working with college admissions personnel, colleges value seeing the details of what a student knows and is able to do. Many college admissions officers have stated to us that they gain much more understanding of a student's abilities with a standards-based report card rather than a simple letter grade or percentage score. Further, colleges value the alignment of standards-based report cards with statewide standards, understanding that these criteria lend legitimacy to a grade as opposed to a letter grade that may or may not have schoolwide or districtwide criteria for it. Most colleges and universities are already dealing with student applications that include standards-based report cards and have systems in place to make judgments on college admissions with such information. As more and more schools convert to standards-based reporting, it will become the norm.

How can teachers justify to parents a student not getting a 100 percent if the student mastered the grade-level expectation (score 3.0)?

Behind this question is a larger question: What is a grade? Is a grade a reward for work done or effort, a reward for being "the best in the class"? Or is a grade a measure of a student's performance on a set of priority standards? We, of course, argue for the second question. Some grading systems may rate students in comparison to each other—for example, when grades are established "on a curve." Parents may be most comfortable seeing grades in the form in which they experienced themselves, as a percentage or a letter grade. In a traditional system, a score of 100 percent might very well mean that the student is the most proficient in the class on the work the teacher asks the students to do. But it might also mean that the student who receives 100 percent is adept at playing the "game" of school, getting work in on time, trying hard, connecting with the teacher on a personal level, and behaving well in class. Percentage scores and letter grades sometimes do not reflect what a student knows and is able to do.

A standards-based classroom uses the standards as criteria for establishing student performance scores. The teacher evaluates students against the requirements of the standards, and not against the performance of other students. A student who receives a score of 3.0 on a priority standard has met the requirements of the standard. This is the goal to which we attempt to guide every student. Some students will be able to exceed that score on some standards, but we do not require performance at the level of 3.5 or 4.0.

When teachers convert a 4.0-based score to a letter grade or a percentage score, they offer the potential for parents misunderstanding the meaning of the percentage score or letter grade, since parents are used to seeing such scores as comparing one student to another. But a standards-based score does not do this, and a percentage score or letter grade based on a conversion from a 4.0 score does not either. Because of this potential confusion, we do not advocate for conversion of scores, but we also realize that in many school districts, as they transition to standards-based grades, such conversions will be required. For more information, see page 128.

How will implementation of standards-based grading affect things like the class's top ten or class ranking?

A purely standards-based environment doesn't compare students in their performance to each other. The technical term for this is *norm-referenced performance*. Standards-based learning advocates a criterion-referenced system where student performance is judged against certain criteria—in this case, the standards.

Most do not teach in a purely standards-based environment. The reality is that most school districts still use class rankings or measurements like the top ten to identify top-performing students. In this situation, the district would use a conversion process, such as the ones chapter 6 described (page 121), to convert a 4.0-based score to a letter grade or percentage score, and schools can use these scores to determine class rank or top ten. The larger question will likely emerge about whether an academic score really reflects top student performance and whether other factors, such as student involvement in activities, sports, student government, and the like, should also be factored into such judgments.

Appendix B:
Creation of an Elementary Unit Plan

Figure B.1 demonstrates how teachers can create a unit at the elementary level—in this case, a second-grade mathematics unit. Consider the following proficiency scale, which applies to a priority standard concerning word problems involving money.

Topic: Word Problems With Money	
Score 4.0	In addition to score 3.0 performance, the student demonstrates in-depth inferences and applications that go beyond what was taught.
Score 3.0	The student will: • Solve word problems involving dollar bills, quarters, dimes, nickels, and pennies using symbols appropriately (2.MD.C.8)
Score 2.0	The student will recognize or recall specific vocabulary, such as: • *Dime, dollar bill, nickel, penny, quarter, symbol, value, word problem.* The student will perform basic processes, such as: • Recognize symbols, such as $, ., and ¢ • Recognize or recall the values of dollar bills, quarters, dimes, nickels and pennies

Source: Adapted from Marzano, Yanoski, Hoegh, & Simms, 2013, p. 264.
Source for standards: National Governors Association Center for Best Practices & Council of Chief State School Officers (NGA & CCSSO), 2010b.

Figure B.1: Second-grade mathematics proficiency scale.

Assuming this standard to be a priority standard, the teacher now proceeds to design a unit in which the goal is to move all students to score 3.0, proficiency on the standard.

The next step is to examine the sequencing of learning targets in the scale to understand the learning progression the unit plan must reflect.

This proficiency scale identifies four learning targets. At score 3.0, which includes the standard, students successfully solve word problems involving dollar bills, quarters, dimes, nickels, and pennies using symbols appropriately. Score 2.0 includes the learning target on vocabulary terms, as well as two prerequisite skills as two learning targets—recognizing symbols and recognizing the values of each form of money. It is usually true that the last of these learning targets will be review since this content is commonly taught in kindergarten and first grade. The relationship between the learning targets at 2.0 and at 3.0 is important. Students will need to know the vocabulary terms of each form of money, their associated values, and the proper use of symbols before they can approach application in word problems. Yet the simple knowledge of this content will not necessarily be sufficient for the "leap" to score 3.0 performance. In preparing students to demonstrate proficiency on this priority standard, there will be several stages (represented by some additional "informal" learning targets) that teachers need to insert on the students' journey to score 3.0 performance. Once the students understand the score 2.0 content, they will need to know how to translate a word problem into a method for solution of the problem. Further, it will be important that students understand the basic mathematical operations that will be used in second-grade word problems—addition and subtraction. Generally, these operations are taught first, in a previous unit, and thus these second-graders should approach this unit with that background knowledge. Although the proficiency scale does not specify these as prerequisite skills, they clearly are important, and an experienced teacher would take into account the need to review these skills as necessary and to connect the new content, solving word problems with addition and subtraction, with the prior knowledge. This will need to be reflected in the unit plan as well (see figure B.2, based on Marzano, 2017).

Day One	Introduce learning goals and proficiency scale. (LG)
	Present the topic of word problems with money. Demonstrate importance of applying addition and subtraction with money. (DI)
	Review key vocabulary terms: *dime, dollar bill, nickel, penny, quarter, symbol, value, word problem*. For new terms, provide examples and non-examples to clarify the terms. (DI)
	Review key symbols: $, ., and ¢. (DI)
Day Two	Review content from day one (DI)
	Conduct activity in which students identify the value of each form of money. (PD)
	Play game to provide guided practice on the value of each form of money. (PD)
	Homework—independent practice in identifying the value of each form of money. (All)

Day Three	Give a quiz on vocabulary and symbols. (Assessment)
	Remind students of learning goal and proficiency scale. Relate work done on days one and two to the proficiency scale. (LG)
	Review content from days one and two. (All)
	Review and correct homework. (All)
	Model process for converting from word problem to addition and subtraction algorithm. (DI)
	Engage students in guided practice in applying process for converting word problem to addition and subtraction. (PD)
	Homework—independent practice (two problems) applying process for converting word problem to addition and subtraction. (All)
Day Four	Have students assess their current level of knowledge relative to the proficiency scale. (Assessment)
	Review and correct homework problems. (All)
	Model process for solving word problems with money. (DI)
	Engage students in guided practice for word problems with money. (PD)
	Homework—independent practice for word problems with money. (All)
Day Five	Remind students about learning goals and proficiency scales. (LG)
	Review work so far in the unit. (DI)
	Engage students in a game applying process for solving word problems with money. (PD)
	Have students assess their current level of knowledge relative to the proficiency scale. (Assessment)
Day Six	Conduct a quiz on solving word problems with money. (Assessment)
	Engage students in an activity involving practice solving word problems with money. (PD)
Day Seven	Organize students for activity requiring them to work in pairs to solve word problems beyond the standard (for example, students must count back change for values up to $10.00). (KA)
Day Eight	Remind students about the learning goals and proficiency scales. (LG)
	Have students assess their current level of knowledge relative to the proficiency scale. (Assessment)
	Engage students in a game in which they must individually apply solutions to word problems involving larger amounts. (Assessment)

Source: Adapted from Marzano, 2017, pp. 107–108.

Figure B.2: Sample unit plan for word problems with money.

A review of this basic unit plan reveals several things. First, the teacher once again assesses often, and the data is used by both the teacher and students to measure progress on the learning progression represented by the proficiency scale. Adjustments to the sequence of the unit, the kind of instruction, and the learning process used by the students can be made at any point in the unit. Note also how often the proficiency scale is "front and center" of the class. It remains the reference point for all feedback to students, for every lesson along the learning progression, and for student self-assessment. This is an important feature of standards-based learning. Research has demonstrated the impact of student goal setting and tracking of progress toward these individual goals. It is well worth the class time to show students their own progress on their goals.

References and Resources

ACT. (2017). *2017/2018: The ACT test user handbook for educators.* Accessed at www
.act.org/content/dam/act/unsecured/documents/ACT-UserHandbook.pdf on April 16, 2018.

Ames, C. (1992). Classrooms: Goals, structures, and student motivation. *Journal of Educational Psychology, 84*(3), 261–271.

Averill, O. H., & Rinaldi, C. (2011). Multi-tier system of supports: A description of RTI and PBIS models for district administrators. *District Administration, 47*(8), 91.

Bangert-Drowns, R. L., Kulik, C. C., Kulik, J. A., & Morgan, M. (1991). The instructional effects of feedback in test-like events. *Review of Educational Research, 61*(2), 213–238.

Barile, N. (2015, January 20). 10 tips for setting successful goals with students. *Education Week Teacher.* Accessed at www.edweek.org/tm/articles/2015/01/20/10-tips-for -setting-successful-goals-with.html on April 16, 2018.

Batsche, G., Elliott, J., Graden, J., Grimes, J., Kovaleski, J., Prasse, D., et al. (2005). *Response to intervention: Policy considerations and implementation.* Alexandria, VA: National Association of State Directors of Special Education.

Batsche, G. M., Kavale, K. A., & Kovaleski, J. F. (2006). Competing views: A dialogue on response to intervention. *Assessment for Effective Intervention, 32*(1), 6–19.

Berry, B., Daughtrey, A., & Wieder, A. (2010, January). *Teacher leadership: Leading the way to effective teaching and learning.* Accessed at https://files.eric.ed.gov/fulltext /ED509719.pdf on December 18, 2017.

Biggs, J. (1998). Assessment and classroom learning: A role for summative assessment? *Assessment in Education, 5*(1), 103–110.

Brookhart, S. M. (2008). *How to give effective feedback to your students.* Alexandria, VA: Association for Supervision and Curriculum Development.

Brookhart, S. M. (2017). *How to give effective feedback to your students* (2nd ed.). Alexandria, VA: Association for Supervision and Curriculum Development.

Buffum, A., Mattos, M., & Malone, J. (2018). *Taking action: A handbook for RTI at work.* Bloomington, IN: Solution Tree Press.

Butler, D. L., & Winne, P. H. (1995). Feedback and self-regulated learning: A theoretical synthesis. *Review of Educational Research, 65,* 245–281.

Butler, R. (1987). Task-involving and ego-involving properties of evaluation: Effects of different feedback conditions on motivational perceptions, interest and performance. *Journal of Educational Psychology, 79*(4), 474–482.

Chapman, C., & Vagle, N. (2011). *Motivating students: 25 strategies to light the fire of engagement.* Bloomington, IN: Solution Tree Press.

College Board AP. (2014). *English literature and composition: Course description.* Accessed at http://media.collegeboard.com/digitalServices/pdf/ap/ap-english-literature-and -composition-course-description.pdf on April 16, 2018.

Conzemius, A. E., & O'Neill, J. (2013). *The handbook for SMART school teams: Revitalizing best practices for collaboration* (2nd ed.). Bloomington, IN: Solution Tree Press.

Danielson, C. (2007). *Enhancing professional practice: A framework for teaching* (2nd ed.). Alexandria, VA: Association for Supervision and Curriculum Development.

Daro, P., Mosher, F., & Corcoran, T. (2011). *Learning trajectories in mathematics: A foundation for standards, curriculum, assessment, and instruction* (Research Report #RR-68). Philadelphia: Consortium for Policy Research in Education.

DuFour, R., & Marzano, R. J. (2011). *Leaders of learning: How district, school, and classroom leaders improve student achievement.* Bloomington, IN: Solution Tree Press.

Dweck, C. S. (2006). *Mindset: The new psychology of success.* New York: Random House.

Dweck, C. S. (2010). Even geniuses work hard. *Educational Leadership, 68*(1), 16–20.

Elawar, M. C., & Corno, L. (1985). A factorial experiment in teachers' written feedback on student homework: Changing teacher behavior a little rather than a lot. *Journal of Educational Psychology, 77*(2), 162–173.

Epstein, J. L. (1988). Effective schools or effective students: Dealing with diversity. In R. Haskins & D. MacRae, Jr. (Eds.), *Child and family policy, vol. 6. Policies for America's public schools: Teachers, equity, and indicators* (pp. 89–126). Norwood, NJ: Ablex.

Farrell, C. C., Marsh, J. A., & Bertrand, M. (2015). Are we motivating students with data? *Educational Leadership, 73*(3), 16–21.

Fisher, D., & Frey, N. (2007). *Checking for understanding: Formative assessment techniques for your classroom.* Alexandria, VA: Association for Supervision and Curriculum Development.

Fisher, D., & Frey, N. (2012). Making time for feedback. *Educational Leadership, 70*(1), 42–46.

Fisher, D., & Frey, N. (2016). *The Fit Teaching approach.* Accessed at www.ascd.org /professional-development/fit-teaching-defined.aspx on April 16, 2018.

Fisher, D., Frey, N., & Hite, S. A. (2016). *Intentional and targeted teaching: A framework for teacher growth and leadership.* Alexandria, VA: Association for Supervision and Curriculum Development.

Fuchs, L. S., & Fuchs, D. (1986). Effects of systematic formative evaluation: A meta-analysis. *Exceptional children, 53*(3), 199–208.

Gareis, C. R., & Grant, L. W. (2008). *Teacher-made assessments: How to connect curriculum, instruction, and student learning*. Larchmont, NY: Eye on Education.

Great Schools Partnership. (2014). *The glossary of educational reform*. Accessed at www .edglossary.org on April 16, 2018.

Greenwood, S., Perrin, A., & Duggan, M. (2016, November 11). *Social media update 2016: Facebook usage and engagement is on the rise, while adoption of other platforms holds steady*. Washington, DC: Pew Research Center. Accessed at www.pewinternet .org/2016/11/11/social-media-update-2016 on April 16, 2018.

Guskey, T. R., & Bailey, J. M. (2001). *Developing grading and reporting systems for student learning*. Thousand Oaks, CA: Corwin Press.

Harlacher, J. E. (2015). *Designing effective classroom management*. Bloomington, IN: Marzano Resources.

Hattie, J. (2009). *Visible learning: A synthesis of over 800 meta-analyses relating to achievement*. New York: Routledge.

Hattie, J., & Timperley, H. (2007). The power of feedback. *Review of Educational Research, 77*(1), 81–112.

Heflebower, T., Hoegh, J. K., & Warrick, P. (2014). *A school leader's guide to standards-based grading*. Bloomington, IN: Marzano Resources.

Heflebower, T., Hoegh, J. K., & Warrick, P. (2017). Get it right the first time! *Kappan, 98*(6), 58–62.

Heritage, M. (2008). *Learning progressions: Supporting instruction and formative assessment*. Washington, DC: Council of Chief State School Officers.

Hoerr, T. R. (2014, September). Principal connection/Goals that matter. *Educational Leadership, 72*(1), 83–84.

International Baccalaureate Organization. (2013). *What is an IB education?* Accessed at www.ibo. org/globalassets/digital-tookit/brochures/what-is-an-ib-education-en.pdf on April 16, 2018.

Jordan, M. (1994). *I can't accept not trying: Michael Jordan on the pursuit of excellence* (M. Vancil, Ed.). New York: HarperCollins.

Kagan, S. (1994). *Cooperative learning*. San Clemente, CA: Kagan.

Kallick, B., & Zmuda, A. (2017). *Students at the center: Personalized learning with habits of mind*. Alexandria, VA: Association for Supervision and Curriculum Development.

Kurt, S. (n.d.). *Dick and Carey instructional model*. Accessed at https://educational technology.net/dick-and-carey-instructional-model on April 16, 2018.

Lemov, D. (2010). *Teach like a champion: 49 techniques that put students on the path to college*. San Francisco, CA: Jossey-Bass.

Locke, E. A., & Bryan, J. F. (1966). Cognitive aspects of psychomotor performance: The effects of performance goals on level of performance. *Journal of Applied Psychology, 50*(4), 286–291.

Locke, E. A., & Latham, G. P. (1990). *A theory of goal-setting and task performance*. Englewood Cliffs, NJ: Prentice Hall.

Locke, E. A., & Latham, G. P. (2002). Building a practically useful theory of goal setting and task performance: A 35-year odyssey. *American Psychologist, 57*(9), 705–717.

Marsh, J. A., Farrell, C. C., & Bertrand, M. (2014). Trickle-down accountability: How middle school teachers engage students in data use. *Educational Policy*, *30*(2), 243–280.

Marzano, R. J. (2003). *What works in schools: Translating research into* action. Alexandria, VA: Association for Supervision and Curriculum Development.

Marzano, R. J. (2006). *Classroom assessment & grading that work*. Alexandria, VA: Association for Supervision and Curriculum Development.

Marzano, R. J. (2009). The art and science of teaching/When students track their progress. *Educational Leadership*, *67*(4), 86–87.

Marzano, R. J. (2010). *Formative assessment & standards-based grading*. Bloomington, IN: Marzano Resources.

Marzano, R. J. (2016). *The Marzano compendium of instructional strategies*. Accessed at www.marzanoresources.com/online-compendium-product on April 16, 2018.

Marzano, R. J. (2017). *The new art and science of teaching*. Bloomington, IN: Solution Tree Press.

Marzano, R. J. (2018). *Making classroom assessments reliable & valid*. Bloomington, IN: Solution Tree Press.

Marzano R. J., & Haystead, M. W. (2008). *Making standards useful in the classroom*. Alexandria, VA: Association for Supervision and Curriculum Development.

Marzano, R. J., Heflebower, T., Hoegh, J. K., Warrick, P., & Grift, G. (with Heckler, L., & Wills, J.). (2016). *Collaborative teams that transform schools: The next step in PLCs*. Bloomington, IN: Marzano Resources.

Marzano, R. J., Norford, J. S., Finn, M., & Finn, D., III. (with Mestaz, R., & Selleck, R.). (2017). *A handbook for personalized competency-based education*. Bloomington, IN: Marzano Resources.

Marzano, R. J., & Pickering, D. J. (with Heflebower, T.). (2011). *The highly engaged classroom*. Bloomington, IN: Marzano Resources.

Marzano, R. J., Warrick, P. B., Rains, C. L., & DuFour, R. (2019). *Leading a high reliability school*. Bloomington, IN: Solution Tree Press.

Marzano, R. J., Warrick, P. B., & Simms, J. A. (with Livingston, D., Livingston, P., Pleis, F., Heflebower, T., Hoegh, J. K., & Magaña, S.). (2014). *A handbook for high reliability schools: The next step in school reform*. Bloomington, IN: Solution Tree Press.

Marzano, R. J., Yanoski, D. C., Hoegh, J. K., & Simms, J. A. (with Heflebower, T., & Warrick, P. B.). (2013). *Using common core standards to enhance classroom instruction & assessment*. Bloomington, IN: Marzano Resources.

Meece, J. L., Anderman, E. M., & Anderman, L. H. (2006). Classroom goal structure, student motivation, and academic achievement. *Annual Review of Psychology*, *57*(1), 487–503.

Miller, J. K. (2015). Four keys for students as data stakeholders. *ASCD Express*, *11*(5). Accessed at www.ascd.org/ascd-express/vol11/1105-miller.aspx on April 16, 2018.

Moss, C. M., & Brookhart, S. M. (2009). *Advancing formative assessment in every classroom: A guide for instructional leaders*. Alexandria, VA: Association for Supervision and Curriculum Development.

National Governors Association Center for Best Practices & Council of Chief State School Officers. (2010a). *Common Core State Standards for English language arts & literacy in history/*

social studies, science, and technical subjects. Washington, DC: Authors. Accessed at www.corestandards.org/assets/CCSSI_ELA%20Standards.pdf on August 27, 2018.

National Governors Association Center for Best Practices & Council of Chief State School Officers. (2010b). *Common Core State Standards for mathematics.* Washington, DC: Authors. Accessed at www.corestandards.org/assets/CCSSI_Math%20Standards.pdf on June 1, 2018.

Nuthall, G. (2005). The cultural myths and realities of classroom teaching and learning: A personal journey. *Teachers College Record, 107*(5), 895–934.

O'Connor, K. (2009). *How to grade for learning K–12* (3rd ed.). Thousand Oaks, CA: Corwin.

Ogle, D. M. (1986). K-W-L: A teaching model that develops active reading of expository text. *Reading Teacher, 39*(6), 564–570.

Pintrich, P. R. (2003). A motivational science perspective on the role of student motivation in learning and teaching contexts. *Journal of Educational Psychology, 95*(4), 667–686.

Pope, D. (2010). Beyond "doing school": From "stressed-out" to "engaged in learning." *Education Canada, 50*(1), 4–8.

Ross, J. A., Hogaboam-Gray, A., & Rolheiser, C. (2002). Student self-evaluation in grade 5–6 mathematics: Effects on problem-solving achievement. *Educational Assessment, 8*(1), 43–59.

Scott, D., & Marzano, R. J. (2014). *Awaken the learner: Finding the source of effective education.* Bloomington, IN: Marzano Resources.

Scriffiny, P. L. (2008). Seven reasons for standards-based grading. *Educational Leadership, 66*(2), 70–74.

Seifert, T. (2004). Understanding student motivation. *Educational Research, 46*(2), 137–149.

Simms, J. A. (2016). *The critical concepts.* Centennial, CO: Marzano Resources.

South Side Middle School. (2017). *Rockville Centre Public Schools MYP rubrics guide 2017–2018.* Accessed at www.ssms.rvcschools.org/UserFiles/Servers/Server_496833/File/MYP%20Info/SSMS_-_MYP_Rubrics_Guide_2017-2018.pdf on July 23, 2018.

Stephanie. (2015, August 5). Item response theory: Simple definition. In *StatisticsHowTo.com*. Accessed at www.statisticshowto.com/item-response-theory on April 18, 2018.

Stiggins, R. J. (2008). *An introduction to student-involved assessment for learning* (5th ed.). Upper Saddle River, NJ: Pearson.

Stony Brook University (2014, April 28). Success breeds success, study confirms. *ScienceDaily.* Accessed at www.sciencedaily.com/releases/2014/04/140428154838.htm on April 16, 2018.

Strauss, V. (2013, July 25). How much time do school districts spend on standardized testing? This much. *The Washington Post.* Accessed at www.washingtonpost.com/news/answer-sheet/wp/2013/07/25/how-much-time-do-school-districts-spend-on-standardized-testing-this-much/?utm_term=.69d517d97254 on April 16, 2018.

Turkay, S. (2014). *Setting goals: Who, why, how?* Accessed at http://hilt.harvard.edu/files/hilt/files/settinggoals.pdf on April 16, 2018.

Weick, K. E., Sutcliffe, K. M., & Obstfeld, D. (1999). Organizing for high reliability: Process of collective mindfulness. *Research in Organizational Behavior, 1*, 81–123.

Wiggins, G. P. (1993). *Assessing student performance: Exploring the purpose and limits of testing.* San Francisco: Jossey-Bass.

Wiggins, G. P. (1996). Honesty and fairness: Toward better grading and reporting. In T. R. Guskey (Ed.), *Communicating student learning: The 1996 ASCD yearbook* (pp. 141–177). Alexandria, VA: Association for Supervision and Curriculum Development.

Wiggins, G. P., & McTighe, J. (2008). *Understanding by design* (2nd ed.). Alexandria, VA: Association for Supervision and Curriculum Development.

Wiliam, D. (2011) *Embedded formative assessment.* Bloomington, IN: Solution Tree Press.

Wilson, L. O. (n.d.). *Madeline Hunter lesson plan model: Or drill that skill—A model of repetition and direct instruction.* Accessed at https://thesecondprinciple.com/teaching-essentials/models-of-teaching/madeline-hunter-lesson-plan-model on April 16, 2018.

Zimmerman, B. J., Bandura, A., & Martinez-Pons, M. (1992). Self-motivation for academic attainment: The role of self-efficacy beliefs and personal goal setting. *American Educational Research Journal, 29*(3), 663–676.

Zimmerman, B. J., & Kitsantas, A. (1997). Developmental phases in self-regulation: Shifting from process goals to outcome goals. *Journal of Educational Psychology, 89*(1), 29–36.

Zimmerman, B. J., & Martinez-Pons, M. (1988). Construct validation of a strategy model of student self-regulated learning. *Journal of Educational Psychology, 80*(3), 284–290.

Index

Professional Development Designed for Success

Empower your staff to tap into their full potential as educators. As an all-inclusive research-into-practice resource center, we are committed to helping your school or district become highly effective at preparing every student for his or her future.

Choose from our wide range of customized professional development opportunities for teachers, administrators, and district leaders. Each session offers hands-on support, personalized answers, and accessible strategies that can be put into practice immediately.

Bring Marzano Resources experts to your school for results-oriented training on:

▶ Assessment & Grading

▶ Curriculum

▶ Instruction

▶ School Leadership

▶ Teacher Effectiveness

▶ Student Engagement

▶ Vocabulary

▶ Competency-Based Education

LEARN MORE at MarzanoResources.com/PD